The Borderline Personality Disorder Workbook

An Integrative Program To Understand And Manage Your BPD

Daniel J. Fox, PhD

16pt

Read How You Want

LARGE PRINT BOOKS, BRAILLE & DAISY

Copyright Page from the Original Book

TABLE OF CONTENTS

"*The Borderline Personality Disorder Workbook* by Daniel Fox is a user-friendly, systematic, and pragmatic set of tools designed to help clients with borderline personality symptoms identify and work toward change through a variety of multidimensional activities and exercises. Supplemented by extensive online content, the positive approach of this workbook is sure to inspire hope for the most discouraged of clients."

—Sherry Cormier, PhD, professor emerita in the department of counseling and counseling psychology at West Virginia University, author of *Counseling Strategies and Interventions for Professional Helpers* and *Sweet Sorrow,* and coauthor of *Interviewing and Change Strategies for Helpers*

"Daniel Fox has bridged the gap between the classic understanding and contemporary application of the authoritative findings concerning personality pathology. In his latest book, Fox has unraveled the dual construct of personality development toward more accurate identification and effective intervention—now and for future generations. The inclusion of the information addressing online behavioral expression is timely and crucial for a culture driven by social media. Online users have practical tools to alert them to unsuspected predators, and/or dating prospects who may have underlying personality pathology. The academic, mental health, and social communities will be forever indebted to Fox."

—Verdi Rountree Lethermon, PhD, retired director of the Houston Police Department's psychological services division, previous adjunct professor at the University of St. Thomas and Houston Baptist University, and private practice clinician

"Daniel Fox won't let you off easy. *The Borderline Personality Disorder Workbook* is truly a book that expects you to WORK! If you think you might have some symptoms of borderline personality disorder (BPD), and are willing to address these problems, and, most of all, are truly committed to working hard at fixing them, this is the book you need."

—Jerold J. Kreisman, MD, author of *Talking to a Loved One with Borderline Personality Disorder,* and coauthor of *I Hate You-Don't Leave Me*

"When working with clients who present with personality disorders, it is sometimes difficult for our clients to grasp the concept of a personality disorder, and even more difficult for them to acquire, execute, and maintain the skills necessary to successfully navigate their everyday lives. As a psychologist and mental health professional, I am always seeking better and more efficient resources that assist my clients on their journey in therapy, as well as providing some structure when developing treatment plans. Well, I hit the jackpot with this resource! Fox has done a marvelous job creating a resource that really helps to better facilitate this work! This workbook is user friendly and can either be used while someone is currently in treatment with a mental health professional, or independently attempting to improve their lives. This workbook does an excellent job breaking down the who, what, when, where, and how of navigating the diagnosis of BPD, and will definitely be an excellent addition to my referral resources for both clinicians and patients!"

—**Meagan N. Houston, PhD,** licensed psychologist; owner of Houston Behavioral Health, PLLC; police psychologist for the Houston Police Department located in Houston, TX; and author of *Treating Suicidal Clients and Self-Harm Behaviors*

"Fox has created an outstanding, comprehensive workbook for individuals suffering from BPD that is both accessible and inviting. It provides a straightforward approach to developing the skills and understanding needed to overcome this painful and emotionally crippling disorder. If you suffer from BPD, this book offers you a clear path toward creating stable and meaningful relationships, developing a compassionate and clearer understanding of yourself, and shedding your feelings of being alone and hopeless. This book will make lives better!"

—Russ Wood, PhD, founder and director of Clear Fork Psychology Services; has treated individuals suffering from BPD and other personality disorders since the 1980s

"Fox has written a superb book that helps both people with borderline personality and the therapists who work with this disorder. In this workbook, Fox lucidly integrates evidence-based techniques and tools to help with thoughts, emotions, behaviors, and relationships—treating those with borderline personality as whole people who can achieve and maintain success and recovery. Fox's work is a must-have for those who want to understand, treat, and recover from borderline personality. Enthusiastically recommended!"

—Lane Pederson, PsyD, author of *The Expanded Dialectical Behavior Therapy Skills Training Manual, Dialectical Behavior Therapy,* and *DBT Skills Training for Integrated Dual Disorder Treatment Settings*

"Daniel Fox has taken his extensive knowledge of this challenging clinical population and has synthesized the literature with his own therapeutic experience and style. *The Borderline Personality Disorder Workbook* challenges the individual with this disorder to change through a series of self-examination exercises of one's beliefs and behaviors, and why these behaviors are maintained. Through a systematic process of exploring what BPD is, to understanding the nature of the problem and acting on what has been learned, the person with BPD is guided to conquering their conflicts and building and eventually maintaining a new self. The workbook may also be used by mental health professionals working with persons with the challenge of BPD."

—**Roy H. Tunick, EdD,** licensed psychologist in West Virginia; past president of the West Virginia Psychological Association (WVPA); and professor emeritus in the department of counseling, rehabilitation counseling, and counseling psychology at West Virginia University

This book is dedicated to my three heartbeats: my wife, Lydia, and my two children, Alexandra and Sebastian

Acknowledgments

A huge thank you to the following individuals for all of their insight and help throughout this process:

Elizabeth Hollis Hansen for all of your help and assistance.

Clancy Drake for your thoughtful suggestions and edits on multiple versions.

Dr. Russ Wood for your insight and suggestions.

Katherine Fox (no relation to author) for your invaluable early edits and feedback.

James Lainsbury for your terrific copyediting and useful feedback.

INTRODUCTION

A New Way to See Borderline Personality Disorder (BPD)

Borderline personality disorder (BPD) was once seen as a disorder that defied treatment. Many individuals who meet criteria for this disorder, as well as those who have traits, are still inclined to believe this even today. However, this is not the case! BPD is a treatable disorder, and with proper treatment, skill building, enhancement of insight, and many other factors we'll discuss and explore throughout this workbook, you can put yourself on a path to reducing BPD's impact and growing beyond it.

The hope for change can be a scary thing, and it may feel like a risk to have hope that something that has been with you for so long could be weakened. I have spent the majority of my career trying to educate mental health professionals, clients, and clients' friends, family members, and significant others that it's possible to successfully treat BPD.

As you go through this workbook, challenge yourself to see yourself and your BPD differently. Encourage yourself to see it as a treatable disorder, something you can grow beyond with the right treatment and skills.

What Can This Workbook Do for You?

There is no "cure" for any personality disorder. A cure implies getting rid of the disease or illness, and we can't get rid of your personality or personality disorder. *Wait! Don't slam the workbook shut yet!* There are different ways to define the successful treatment of a personality disorder. What we can do is reduce symptoms and their impact on you, others, and situations. This workbook will help you do just that by giving you the skills and tools to act and react to your world in a more productive manner; to learn about what drives what we'll call negative beliefs, behaviors, and patterns; and to reduce the intrusiveness of BPD symptoms and the impact they have on your life.

Not a "One and Done" Deal

There are many great skills, tools, activities, and exercises in this workbook that'll help you reduce the negative impact of BPD and the negative beliefs, behaviors, and patterns you engage in that are connected to it. None of them are "one and done" skills or exercises. I often tell my clients that learning a mental health skill for managing BPD, or any other mental health concern, is similar to learning how to roller skate. At first it may seem odd and you may stumble, but the more you do it the better you'll get. You may find that there isn't enough space in this workbook for you to fully answer the exercise prompts and questions. Please don't let this stop you from writing and thinking! Use as much extra paper as you need to complete these. Many of the exercises can be downloaded at ht tp://www.newharbinger.com/42730. See the back of the book for details about accessing this material.

Learning to use skills and tools takes time and practice. I encourage you to integrate them—and the adaptive and healthy beliefs, behaviors, and patterns they bring—into your everyday life. Doing so will require commitment and work, but the outcome will be less intrusion of BPD in your life, which can build your sense of empowerment and significantly impact your life.

How This Workbook Is Organized

This workbook is organized in five sections based upon my therapeutic approach to working with individuals who exhibit varying degrees of BPD symptoms. In part 1 you'll learn what BPD is, how common it is, how it develops, and what symptoms of the disorder you tend to exhibit. We'll explore your connection to and comfort with others, as well as the different types of BPD.

In part 2 you'll learn about your readiness and motivation to participate in growing beyond BPD and determine where you are in the process of change. You'll also learn about common triggers that promote maladaptive (unhealthy) behaviors and beliefs, and I'll provide you with the skills to help you recognize whether your relationships are positive or negative.

In part 3 you'll learn to manage your responses when you're triggered, to recognize high-risk situations, and to cultivate options for yourself for adaptive coping. You'll acquire the skills to change and challenge those dysfunctional beliefs, learn self-soothing techniques to enhance personal control, and strengthen love and conflict resolution skills.

In part 4 we'll go over the tools you can use to reconstruct and build a healthier view of yourself and the people (and situations) who encourage adaptive and healthy response patterns. This part of the book will guide you toward identifying your internal motivations and perceptual distortions; challenging your destructive feelings, beliefs, and wishes; and examining the internal defense mechanisms that prevent psychological growth and perpetuate BPD symptoms. You'll confront your internal love-hate relationship and be encouraged and challenged to give up your "old ways" and to welcome new adaptive and healthy response patterns.

In part 5 you'll learn about the types of stress you experience and implement the best coping strategy for dealing with them. This will help you build upon your newly found self-acceptance, as well as maintain the insights, tools, skills, and awareness of your past, present, and future that you've gained from the work you'll have done in this book.

There is extensive online content to help strengthen the skills you develop from this workbook. All five parts of this workbook have online summaries that pull together the concepts and skills from the chapters in each part. Please use them, because they will reinforce the growth you've made. These accessories, as well as other material for the book, are available for download at http://www.newharbinger. com/42730.

How to Use This Workbook

This workbook is designed for individuals with BPD, or for those with BPD traits who may not meet the full criteria for the diagnosis but have issues similar to people with BPD. Regardless of which camp you fall in, this book is absolutely for anyone who wants to reduce their problems related to this disorder. You can use this workbook as an additional component to treatment or as a singular resource. It's always good to have a positive resource and outlet in life who can support you when you need it, such as a mental health provider. If you aren't seeing a therapist, I encourage you to consider doing so.

Throughout this workbook I'll refer to Betty and Tony, and we'll look at their experiences learning and using the skills outlined in this workbook. These two individuals and their stories are based upon a combination of past clients I've had in treatment. They're here to illustrate skills and to make concepts easier to understand.

One great thing about workbooks is that you can go at your own pace. You can address issues as you feel ready to address them. The material in this workbook is designed to help you do that by identifying your motivation, then behaviors, then the internal drives and needs that promote your BPD, and finally ways to maintain the skills you've learned and the successes you've experienced while going through the workbook. Start at the beginning and work forward, and go as far as you feel comfortable. You can always learn some skills, put the workbook down for a bit, and then, when you feel ready to go further, pick it back up again.

When and How to Get HELP

If you feel triggered or overwhelmed while working on something in this workbook, you can try using the strategies you've learned and practiced or you can seek assistance from a trusted person, which may be a mental health provider. As you go through this workbook, it's important to keep in mind that addressing and exploring BPD may bring up many issues for you that you can't manage on your own. If you have thoughts of self-harm or of harming others, stop!

Contact your mental health provider,

call the national suicide hotline (1–800–273–8255), or

go to the nearest emergency room.

Your safety is priority #1.

BPD is a challenging disorder, and difficult thoughts, feelings, and memories may come up as you go through this workbook. It's vital to know when you may need help. To assist you with this, I created the HELP steps:

H—When you *have* intense emotions, thoughts, or memories,

E—*Exit* the situation or consider another way to deal with them instead of reacting negatively.

L— *Let* s—p yourself, and relax.

P—*Pursue* help from a trusted and positive friend or mental health provider if the intensity of your emotions, thoughts, or memories isn't reduced and you feel pressured to harm yourself or others.

If emotions, thoughts, and memories overwhelm you, remember to use the HELP steps.

PART 1

BPD and Successful Treatment

CHAPTER 1

BPD 101

Many people misunderstand what borderline personality disorder (BPD) is and how it impacts people's lives, including those who have it and the family members, friends, loved ones, coworkers, and others who are in their life. Perhaps you were diagnosed by a mental health professional, or, having felt that something just wasn't quite right in your life, you researched BPD and found that some of its symptoms seem to reflect how you see yourself, others, and situations. In this chapter we're going to clear away the clutter and confusion and identify the criteria that fit for you. Getting a clear picture of your BPD is the start of a journey of self-exploration, which will allow you to grow beyond your BPD.

As you already know, BPD shows up differently for different people. So to start, I'd like to introduce you to Betty. Betty struggled with BPD for many years, but she was able to overcome it by developing an understanding and skills that empowered her to take control of her BPD symptoms and her life. We're going to talk about her a lot as we make our way through this workbook.

Betty

Betty was a twenty-two-year-old woman who had always had difficulty making and keeping friends. Multiple relationships with friends, significant others, family members, and coworkers had ended because of intense arguments and even physical fights. Many people were frustrated with her strong need to control them and dictate what they did, her demanding style, and her immediate and intense reactions. In many ways she was like a chameleon, as she tended to change her views and values to fit in with the different types of people, such as people who liked politics, were part of the goth subculture, or were sexually adventurous. She changed to avoid being rejected and to feel understood.

If her friends wanted to do something other than what she wanted, Betty often became visibly angry and then ditched them. Yet her friends also enjoyed spending time with her because she was usually the life of the party and never backed down from a dare. However, sometimes Betty was slow to respond to her friends' texts or emails and would stay at home for days at a time for no obvious reason. She'd regularly say, "I'm usually alone in a crowded room." When she wasn't around friends, Betty often cried and searched the Internet for her next romantic encounter.

Betty was head over heels in love with Steven the instant they met and wanted to talk with him every day. She broke up with him when he didn't immediately respond to her texts about a gift she'd left on his doorstep. She began referring to him as "the devil." This was a difficult breakup for Betty, and though she ended it she felt rejected, alone, lost, conflicted, and confused about her feelings about Steven, as well as about herself.

Betty had issues outside of her relationships, too. When she was highly stressed, she often felt detached from her body and the world around her. She said that she often felt like a puppet with a stranger working her strings. She drove recklessly and had two DWIs, and she shoplifted if things got "too boring." Betty had seen numerous psychologists and psychiatrists since turning twelve years old, and she was diagnosed with obsessive-compulsive personality disorder, impulse control disorder, and major depressive disorder. Medication was helpful for some things, but not for others. Her problems persisted, and medications kept changing as issues arose and dissipated based on what was going on in her life.

After Betty broke up with Steven, she cut her arms and her coworkers saw the scabs. She was embarrassed, and she decided to reenter treatment. This time in therapy she discovered that she met criteria for borderline personality disorder. This diagnosis made sense to her, and having it (and the help of a skilled therapist) allowed her to embark on a journey of healing.

Many of the approaches and techniques you'll find in this workbook helped Betty grow past the harmful patterns of BPD that had been holding her back for so long. They worked for her, and they can work for you, too.

Betty's experience of BPD may resonate with you, but you may be doubtful that you can successfully manage it. Before Betty could manage her BPD, she first had to know what it is and that she wasn't alone in suffering from it. The same is true of you, so let's explore what BPD is and how common it is.

What Is BPD?

BPD is one of ten personality disorders identified in the fifth edition of the *Diagnostic and Statistical Manual of Mental Disorders* (DSM-5; APA 2013). This is the standard reference that therapists of all specialties use to diagnose mental disorders of all kinds. A *personality disorder* is broadly defined by the inability to adjust one's behavior, thinking, and pattern of responses in relation to particular situations or feelings, or both. In the words of the DSM-5, BPD is "a pervasive pattern of instability of interpersonal relationships, self-image, and affects, and marked impulsivity, beginning by early adulthood and present in a variety of contexts" (APA 2013, 663). Many individuals who meet the criteria for BPD can look back at their childhood and adolescence and see the beginning of these symptoms and patterns. However, a diagnosis of BPD is often inappropriate for children and adolescents, because they're still growing and developing and learning how to manage and respond to life circumstances. For someone under the age of eighteen to be diagnosed with a personality disorder, including BPD, their symptoms must have been present for at least one year (APA 2013).

There are nine criteria listed in the DSM-5 related to BPD. An individual needs to meet five or more of these to qualify for the diagnosis. You may have received a diagnosis from a mental health professional, and hopefully that individual went over the criteria that relate specifically to you. To help you gain a clearer understanding of your BPD, the exercise below will help you identify criteria that are specific to you. I paired each with an example from Betty's story.

Identifying Your BPD Symptoms

Place a checkmark next to any description below that matches how you see the world and how you act and react.

☐ Frantic efforts to avoid real or imagined abandonment (APA 2013, 663).

Betty perceived that her boyfriend was abandoning her because he didn't respond to her gift quickly enough, which drove her to break up with him, causing her to feel even more abandoned. She had a history of inappropriate behavior related to feeling abandoned.

☐ A pattern of unstable and intense interpersonal relationships characterized by alternating between extremes of idealization and devaluation (APA 2013, 663).

When Betty met Steven, she was "head over heels" in love and wanted to talk with him every day, but she broke up with him, referring to him as "the devil," when he didn't respond quickly enough to her texts about a gift she'd left on his doorstep. She'd had similar experiences with her three previous boyfriends.

☐ Identity disturbance: markedly and persistently unstable self-image or sense of self (APA 2013, 663).

Betty had difficulty making and keeping friends, as she tended to change the types of people she liked to spend time with, and her views and values changed to match them.

☐ Impulsivity in at least two areas that are potentially self-damaging (for example, spending, sex, substance abuse, reckless driving, binge eating) (APA 2013, 663).

When she wasn't in a relationship, Betty compulsively searched the Internet for her next encounter. She drove recklessly and had two DWIs, and she shoplifted if things got "too boring."

☐ Recurrent suicidal behavior, gestures, or threats, or self-mutilating behavior (APA 2013, 663).

Betty had a history of self-mutilation, cutting her arms or legs when she was under stress or feeling lonely. She cut her arms after breaking up with Steven.

☐ Affective instability due to a marked reactivity of mood (for example, intense episodic dysphoria, irritability, or anxiety usually lasting a few hours and only rarely more than a few days) (APA 2013, 663).

When she wasn't around her friends, Betty often curled up on her bed and cried, or grasped for ways to calm herself and feel connected, such as going on texting sprees or scouring dating sites for her next hookup.

☐ Chronic feelings of emptiness (APA 2013, 663).

Betty often felt alone, even when she was hooking up or was with a significant other. She'd say, "I'm usually alone in a crowded room."

☐ Inappropriate, intense anger or difficulty controlling anger (for example, frequent displays of temper, constant anger, recurrent physical fights) (APA 2013, 663).

Betty had had multiple intense arguments and physical altercations with friends, boyfriends, family members, and coworkers.

☐ Transient, stress-related paranoid ideation or severe dissociative symptoms (APA 2013, 663). (*Paranoid ideation* is being afraid that others are plotting against you, and *dissociation* is mentally separating from physical or emotional experiences, or both.)

When under a high degree of stress, Betty often felt detached from her body and the world around her and reported that she felt like she was a puppet with a stranger working her strings.

Write the number of checkmarks here:

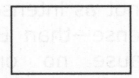

Did you check five or more criteria above (circle your response)?

YES   NO

Based on the exercise above, do you feel that the symptoms of BPD fit with how you see your world, interact with others, and respond to people and situations (circle your response)?

YES   NO

If you marked four criteria or fewer but still identified some BPD traits that you recognize in yourself, this workbook can still be of great value to you. It can help you learn how to reduce the harmful impact they're having in your life.

BPD Is a Spectrum

As you went through the preceding exercise, you may have noticed that some of your behaviors, feelings, and thoughts are not as intense—or perhaps are more intense—than Betty's. That's normal, because no one's BPD is identical to anyone else's. The *intensity* or *severity* of each criterion is unique to each person, as is how it impacts one's life. Betty's behavior as it relates to some of the criteria is severe or extreme, serving as important sources of pain and possibly even danger for her. The same may not be true for you. This difference in presentation is what helps therapists determine where an individual falls on the BPD spectrum, which ranges from mild to extreme.

If Betty is an example of someone who falls at the extreme end of the BPD spectrum, where do you think you fall? In the exercise below, circle where on the spectrum you think you fall for each BPD criterion. Take your time and just answer what feels right for you. There are no right or wrong answers, only what you think, and that's good enough.

Frantic efforts to avoid real or imagined abandonment.

Mild   Moderate   Severe   Extreme

A pattern of unstable and intense interpersonal relationships characterized by alternating between extremes of idealization and devaluation.

Mild   Moderate   Severe   Extreme

Identity disturbance: markedly and persistently unstable self-image or sense of self.

Mild   Moderate   Severe   Extreme

Impulsivity in at least two areas that are potentially self-damaging (for example, spending, sex, substance abuse, reckless driving, binge eating).

Mild   Moderate   Severe   Extreme

Recurrent suicidal behavior, gestures, or threats, or self-mutilating behavior.

Mild   Moderate   Severe   Extreme

Affective instability due to a marked reactivity of mood (for example, intense episodic dysphoria, irritability, or anxiety usually lasting a few hours and only rarely more than a few days).

Mild   Moderate   Severe   Extreme

Chronic feelings of emptiness.

Mild   Moderate   Severe   Extreme

Inappropriate, intense anger or difficulty controlling anger (for example, frequent displays of temper, constant anger, recurrent physical fights).

Mild   Moderate   Severe   Extreme

Transient, stress-related paranoid ideation or severe dissociative symptoms.

Mild   Moderate   Severe   Extreme

When you look at your responses, where would you put yourself on the BPD spectrum?

Mild   Moderate   Severe   Extreme

Now that you've identified the symptoms that impact you the most, the ones that influence how you see yourself, the world around you, and those within it, let's piece together what influenced your answers and describe it below.

Why did you rate yourself (mild, moderate, severe, or extreme) as you did? (You can consider the number of symptoms marked at a particular level, specific symptoms that cause you to judge yourself harshly, and so on.)

_____

_____

_____

_____

In what part or parts of your life (for example, relationships with family and friends, work, how you see yourself, and so on) do these symptoms cause the greatest problems?

_____

_____

_____

When you look back at your responses to the questions above, and your ratings, what have you learned about your BPD?

_____

_____

_____

Learning about and exploring your BPD will help you grow beyond it, but sometimes it can make you feel like you're alone. You may feel like you're the only one having these feelings, thoughts, memories, and reactions, but it's important to remember that you're not alone. BPD is a disorder that many people experience.

How Common Is BPD?

Feeling alone is common for people with BPD—so common that it's a criterion (chronic feelings of emptiness) for the disorder. But you're not alone.

Approximately 18 million—or nearly 6 percent—of adults in the United States have been diagnosed with BPD (Grant et al. 2008). Historically women were diagnosed with BPD more often than men, as much as three to one, but nearly an equal amount of both genders (53 percent women, 47 percent men; Grant et al. 2008) meet the criteria for BPD.

In other parts of the world the prevalence of BPD ranges between 1.4 percent and 5.9 percent of the general population (Samuels et al. 2002; Coid et al. 2006; Lenzenweger et al. 2007; Grant et al. 2008; Trull et al. 2010). As you can see from these statistics, many individuals are dealing with BPD and are working to overcome it.

Setting the Stage for Success

Using the spaces below, pull together what you learned from this chapter so you can take this information with you.

The most helpful information I learned from this chapter:

1. _____

2. _____

3. _____

While going through this chapter, I was thinking _____, and it helped me to see that _____
_____
_____

This workbook is for and about men and women like Betty and you who have to deal with issues related to BPD, be they traits or the full diagnosis. Throughout this workbook I use the term *borderline personality disorder (BPD)* when discussing the thoughts, feelings, reactions, beliefs, and wishes of people who fall somewhere on the BPD spectrum. However, it is *not* my intention to define or label individuals based on this term or diagnosis. It's important to remember that a diagnosis is used for treatment and not for self-definition. It's my hope that you'll find this exploration of BPD to be a route to healing and growth, along which you'll find ways to control and overcome it.

Now that you know more about what BPD is, let's explore its possible roots and causes.

CHAPTER 2

Where Does BPD Come From?

This chapter offers insight into the various causes, or roots, of BPD, including genetic factors, brain differences, psychological and social influences, and early experiences. The exercise I included will help you understand your own history, as well as the history of those in your life who may also exhibit BPD symptoms.

The Roots of BPD

It's common for people with a BPD diagnosis to look inward with a sense of self-blame, self-hate, confusion, and conflict. You may feel as though you're broken or cursed. You may also believe that this disorder is an inescapable result of who you are and what you've experienced. Unfortunately, these beliefs and feelings keep BPD in place, leaving you feeling alone, ashamed, and tangled up in the disorder.

BPD is the most researched and treated personality disorder (Dingfelder 2004) in psychology, yet its causes are neither simple nor certain. There is no single best explanation as to why you display the symptoms of BPD and have the difficulties you do, but it might be helpful for you to explore the areas—genetics, psychological and social influences, and brain functioning—that have the greatest influence on the development of BPD (Benjamin 1996).

Genetics

Research indicates that 37 to 69 percent of BPD diagnoses are related to genetic inheritance (Ahmad et al. 2014; Distel et al. 2008; Gunderson et al. 2011). Individuals who have a first-degree relative (parent, sibling, or child) with a BPD diagnosis are five times more likely to be diagnosed (APA 2013; Gunderson 1994) themselves than those who don't have such a relative. The BPD symptoms—impulsivity, anxiousness, difficulty controlling mood, and problems with interpersonal relationships (Reichborn-Kjennerud et al. 2013; Zanarini et al. 2004)—one displays tend to have a strong family link. For example, if your mom had a tendency to be impulsive, you might as well.

In short, if a close relative has BPD, you're more likely to also display BPD symptoms or to be diagnosed. But keep in mind that we're not simply an expression of our genetics.

Psychological and Social Influences

Many individuals who have been diagnosed with BPD experienced traumatic life events during childhood, such as abuse or abandonment (Ball and Links 2009; MacIntosh, Godbout, and Dubash 2015). Specifically, 36.5 to 67 percent of people diagnosed with BPD experienced sexual abuse (Elzy 2011; McGowan et al. 2012), but neglect, childhood adversity, caregivers with alcohol and drug abuse issues, chaotic family life, disrupted attachments, having lots of different caregivers or unreliable caregivers, and adults who modeled poor emotional control have also been linked to the development of BPD (Dahl 1985; Fonagy, Target, and Gergely 2000; Judd and McGlashan 2003; Linehan 1993).

It's important to note that not everyone who has experienced traumatic life events develops BPD, and not everyone with BPD has experienced them. It's also worth noting that there's a correlation between the severity of abuse, the age it first began, the number of instances of abuse, and the type of abuse (such as sexual, emotional, physical, or psychological) and the future development of BPD (Chanen and Kaess 2012; Yen et al. 2002; Zanarini et al. 2002).

Psychological and social influences together determined your early experiences. How often they occurred, how many you experienced, how severe they were, and at what age they happened can all influence the development of BPD. Although many individuals who develop BPD followed a similar pattern, or sequence, of early experiences, there is no single route to a BPD diagnosis. That said, recognizing a common, or influential, set of experiences can help you better understand your BPD as you continue on this journey.

In her book *Interpersonal Diagnosis and Treatment of Personality Disorders* (1996), Lorna Smith Benjamin identifies a sequence of early experiences that contributes to the development of BPD (see figure 1). If one, two, or even all of these early life experiences happened for you, it doesn't mean that you'll absolutely develop BPD, but you are more likely to exhibit similar beliefs, behaviors, and patterns of individuals with BPD.

How you thought about and reacted to yourself, others, and situations influenced how your brain developed and functions today. Let's now explore brain functioning, the last potential origin of BPD, and then we'll identify the roots of your BPD in the exercise that follows.

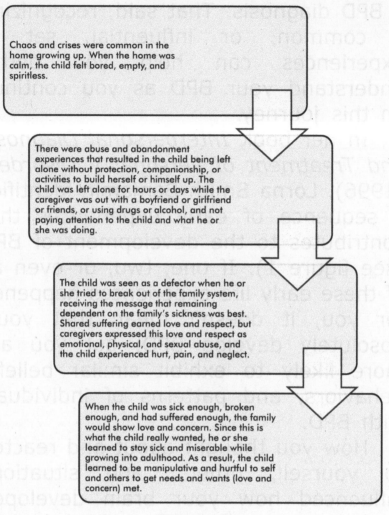

Chaos and crises were common in the home growing up. When the home was calm, the child felt bored, empty, and spiritless.

There were abuse and abandonment experiences that resulted in the child being left alone without protection, companionship, or activities to build herself or himself up. The child was left alone for hours or days while the caregiver was out with a boyfriend or girlfriend or friends, or using drugs or alcohol, and not paying attention to the child and what he or she was doing.

The child was seen as a defector when he or she tried to break out of the family system, receiving the message that remaining dependent on the family's sickness was best. Shared suffering earned love and respect, but caregivers expressed this love and respect as emotional, physical, and sexual abuse, and the child experienced hurt, pain, and neglect.

When the child was sick enough, broken enough, and had suffered enough, the family would show love and concern. Since this is what the child really wanted, he or she learned to stay sick and miserable while growing into adulthood. As a result, the child learned to be manipulative and hurtful to self and others to get needs and wants (love and concern) met.

Figure 1

Brain Functioning

Research has shown that individuals with BPD have similar brain functioning. For people diagnosed with BPD, areas of the brain that impact their ability to control impulses and aggression, to accurately recognize emotional expressions in others, to calm down after getting excited or angry, or to reason through problems when agitated or angry tend to show activity (Goodman et al. 2014; Lenzenweger et al. 2007; Sala et al. 2011; Soloff et al. 2008).

These findings, that individuals with BPD have a brain that functions differently from those who do not have BPD, hasn't been attributed to just one cause. It's believed that the roots of genetics, psychological and social influences, and early experiences play a part in the development and functioning of your brain and how it, and you, act and react when you think about, evaluate, and perceive yourself, others, and situations. This connection is a good thing: if situations, experiences, actions, and reactions influenced how your brain developed and now operates, then you can change your brain functioning by doing things differently, such as employing new strategies to overcome your BPD.

Roots and Influences of Your BPD

The roots that influenced the development of your BPD are as individual as you are, and having insight into how your BPD may have developed can help you control it and grow beyond it. That's why we're now going to explore your roots using an exercise designed to help you determine what percentage of your BPD symptoms are related to genetics, psychological and social influences, and brain functioning.

In the spaces below, identify family members and close relatives who appear to meet the criteria for BPD on the left, and then on the right describe their relationship issues, behaviors, and problems with mood and impulse control that are similar to yours. This can be difficult, because you may not like these individuals very much. Maybe it hurts to associate yourself with them, to feel that your behavior or biology is similar to theirs. This process is important; it will help you recognize your roots and develop the insight and strength to overcome BPD, so it's worth doing.

Family Members	Symptoms

Now that you've identified some people with whom you may share a BPD-related genetic link, let's consider the psychological and social influences and early experiences that may have contributed to the development of your BPD. Make a checkmark next to each item in the list below that seems relevant.

☐ I experienced abuse or abandonment when I was younger.

☐ The abuse I experienced occurred more than two times and was severe.

☐ I was neglected as a child.

☐ I struggled as a child in school.

☐ The following people in my life were inconsistent and not dependable:

☐ Mom

☐ Dad

☐ Brother(s)

☐ Sister(s)

☐ Other family members: _____

☐ Friends

☐ Others: _____

☐ Strangers were often around while I was growing up.

☐ When I had an emotional bond with someone, this person usually broke it and betrayed me.

☐ My parents or caregivers abused alcohol or drugs, or both.

☐ I saw my parents or caregivers act aggressively toward others.

☐ My parents or caregivers acted aggressively toward me.

☐ Chaos and crises were common in my home growing up.

☐ When my home was calm, I felt bored, empty, and spiritless.

☐ When my home was calm, I felt anxious and afraid because something bad was right around the corner.

☐ I was left alone for hours or days at a time without supervision, protection, or companionship.

☐ My parent or caregiver was often out with boyfriends or girlfriends.

☐ My parent or caregiver often used alcohol or drugs, or both, around me.

☐ While growing up, I often felt like no one was paying attention to me and what I was doing. I was on my own.

☐ When I tried to break out of the family cycle, I was seen as a traitor.

☐ I learned from my family that I am loved when I am dependent on them and feel bad about myself.

☐ Love and respect in my home usually meant hurt, pain, neglect, emotional abuse, physical abuse, sexual abuse, or a combination of these.

☐ At my lowest of low points, my family or caregiver showed me some form of love and concern—but only then.

☐ I learned that staying sick and "broken" meant that people would love me.

☐ From my family I learned to be dishonest and devious, because honesty always ended with me "burned" and hurt.

Based on what you explored in this exercise, think about what percentage of your BPD is related to genetics and brain functioning versus psychological and social influences and early experiences. Write these percentages in the blank circles in figure 2; they should add up to 100 percent. This is not a scientific formula, but rather a way to visualize what you learned from this chapter and this exercise.

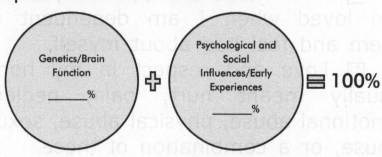

Figure 2

It's unlikely that you wrote 100 percent in only one of the bubbles, because part of you knows that genetics, brain function, psychological and social influences, and early experiences combined make us who we are.

As you remember or uncover these influences, and think about the ways they combined to create BPD, you may feel like you're doomed to always have issues with BPD. This doesn't have to be the case—if it were, no one with unhappy beginnings would ever overcome past hurts. BPD doesn't mean you're destined for loss, suffering, and pain forever. Rather, knowing the roots of the disorder will help you overcome its impact. You have to know where you're from to know where you're going.

Setting the Stage for Success

Using the spaces below, pull together what you learned from this chapter so you can take this information with you.

The most helpful information I learned from this chapter:

1. _____
2. _____
3. _____

While going through this chapter, I was thinking _____, and it helped me to see that _____

_____

Next, we'll explore how a BPD diagnosis affects the emotional and physical bond you create with others, also known as attachment.

CHAPTER 3

Attachment and BPD

Attachment is an emotional motivator we all have inside us that connects us to others. Each of us starts developing a pattern, or type, of attachment in our earliest days based largely on how our caregivers behave toward us. Your attachment style not only influences how you see yourself and the world around you, but also how you act and react in situations. In this chapter you'll learn how attachment types develop and motivate people, identify your own attachment type, and work on skills to form secure and strong relationships. In chapter 1 I introduced you to Betty, and in this chapter you're going to meet Tony and explore his experience with BPD. Throughout the rest of the workbook you'll learn more about Betty and Tony and their challenges growing beyond BPD. You may experience similar challenges as you make your way through this workbook. Let's get to know Tony.

Tony

Tony's mother often told him that he was a burden, a disappointment, and a failure. As early as Tony can remember he wanted his mother to love and care for him, but the harder he tried the more she rejected and scolded him. She put all of her energy into her boyfriends and alcohol. He always wanted to be recognized by her but could never "get it right." He tried very hard in school and got good grades to make her proud, but one time he came home with a report card with As and Bs, and his mother said, "Don't be a show-off. No one likes a know-it-all." This really stuck with him, and he stopped trying to excel in school, a habit he carried forward into college and his first job.

After the report card incident Tony turned his focus to sports. He was a very good baseball player, and coaches really liked him. One coach pulled Tony aside and said that he could help him be even better, but he'd have to practice more, and for longer. Tony declined the extra help because he didn't feel that he was worth the coach's extra time and attention—and being praised made him uneasy and question the coach's motives. Tony always tried to get his mother to come to his games, but she refused—except for one time. At this game, Tony struck out once, got on base twice, and made three runs. When he got home, his mother complained about what a waste of time the game had been. She told him she was embarrassed that he spent his time on a sport he wasn't even good at, because he had struck out whereas many of the other kids hadn't. Tony quit baseball.

Tony really liked his first girlfriend, Pam. After one week together he knew he was in love with her. But he had a feeling she would never love him the same way he loved her. He often asked her how she felt about him and tried to please her by doing things she *liked. He would respond to her texts and emails immediately, so she knew she was a priority. Tony focused all of his time and energy on being close to Pam, rearranging his schedule and responsibilities to be with her while ignoring his other friends. When Pam had other things she needed to do, Tony felt alone, lost, and desperate to be with her, but he was also conflicted, because he didn't feel important enough for her to spend time with. He created "tests" often to prove that she loved him. For example, Tony purposely posted a negative message about himself on Facebook to see if she would defend him. After three hours of checking continuously she still hadn't responded, so Tony drank a bottle of Vodka. Pam found him passed out. Unable to wake him, she called an ambulance.*

Tony was very confused and conflicted about his feelings for Pam. He had developed an insecure attachment type based upon his relationship with his mother and how she treated him. He felt a push and pull inside of him: he was motivated to be close with someone and to feel liked and valued, but he questioned his worthiness to be loved—or to be valued at all. He couldn't really trust that he was genuinely loved and valued because he didn't really believe he was lovable and valuable. This insecure attachment and longing drove his behavior in school, baseball, jobs, and relationships.

How We Develop Our Attachment Type

The degree to which we feel loved growing up affects the development of our self-esteem and self-acceptance and shapes how we seek out love and connect with others. Many animals, from rabbits to human beings, seek to connect with other beings. We call this internal drive to connect *attachment,* and it's with human beings from the first day of life.

The father of attachment theory, John Bowlby, believed that infants possess this desire so they can grow and develop within a safe environment (Bowlby 1971). When caregivers offer babies attention, care, and protection, they feel safe, secure, soothed, and recognized. This allows them to develop a high level of trust and understanding with others and the world around them, and they carry this ability into their relationships as they grow. This is a secure attachment type. People who exhibit this attachment type see themselves as valuable, as important, and as having worth in the world; see others as genuine and caring; and are able to develop and maintain healthy and stable relationships (Bartholomew and Horowitz 1991).

When a baby's caregivers don't meet her need to be seen and cared for, her ability to trust herself and others is compromised. Consider Tony's experience. He tried and tried to develop a loving connection with his mother, but she wasn't willing or able to provide this for him. As a result he developed an insecure attachment type that affected many areas of his life.

Like Tony, perhaps you didn't have a safe and soothing environment growing up and weren't able to develop a secure type of attachment. Having an insecure attachment type increases a person's likelihood of developing problems with anxiety, anger, depression, self-worth, self-esteem, and emotional connection and control (Bowlby 1977). Insecure attachment types are common among people with BPD (Agrawal et al. 2004). There are three types (Bartholomew and Horowitz 1991):

1. *Preoccupied:* Having an intense desire to connect to others
2. *Dismissing:* Disregarding others and their emotions
3. *Fearful:* Wanting to be with others but being afraid one is not worthy of love and affection

Identifying Your Attachment Type

In this exercise you're going to identify your attachment type. In the boxes below, write a checkmark next to the statements that match how you see yourself and feel about your connections to others. You may check off features in several boxes, which is fine. Most people display features of multiple attachment types. When you're done, the box that has the most identified features is your attachment type.

Box 1	Box 2
☐ I find it easy be close to others. ☐ I'm comfortable depending on others. ☐ I'm comfortable with others depending on me. ☐ I'm not worried about not having a close relationship. ☐ I'm okay with others not accepting me.	☐ I'm uncomfortable not being in a close relationship. ☐ I want a lot of intimacy and approval in my relationships. ☐ I worry that others don't value me as much as I value them. ☐ I want complete emotional intimacy with my significant other. ☐ I feel that others don't get as emotionally close as I would like.
Box 3	**Box 4**
☐ I am comfortable not having emotional relationships. ☐ Independence is very important to me. ☐ I don't need anyone else's help to get things done. ☐ I don't see a lot of value in emotional relationships. ☐ I never feel truly close to someone else.	☐ I'm uncomfortable getting close to others. ☐ I want to be close to someone, but I'm afraid of being close. ☐ It's difficult to trust significant others completely. ☐ I'm afraid I'll be hurt if I get too close to someone emotionally. ☐ I feel unworthy of my significant other's time and attention.

Add up the number of checkmarks in each of the four boxes above and write the number in the appropriate box below. For example, if you marked 3 of the 5 statements in box 1, write a 3 in box 1 below.

Box 1	Box 2
Box 3	Box 4

Each box represents one of the four attachment types, and the box with the highest number identifies yours. If you have the same number in more than one box, then you have features of both attachment types. Each of the four attachment types is defined below. Circle the type (or types) that is the best match for you.

Secure (Box 1)	Preoccupied (Box 2)
High self-worth; believes others are approachable and caring; comfortable with autonomy and with forming close relationships.	Self-worth is based on gaining the approval and acceptance of others; relationships are intense, to the point of relying on individuals too much; anxiety is reduced when with a significant other.
Dismissing (Box 3)	**Fearful (Box 4)**
Positive view of self; desires independence and appears to avoid connections with others altogether; denies the need for close relationships and will say relationships are unimportant.	Sees self in a negative way; doesn't trust others; afraid to be in close relationships but feels the need; experiences discomfort with close relationships and sees self as unworthy of responsiveness from a significant other.

People with BPD are likely to develop a preoccupied or fearful attachment type, or both. These two attachment types are similar in that people experience a high degree of anxiety associated with the fear of abandonment, but they differ in how people interact with others in order to feel safe. Individuals with a preoccupied attachment type tend to seek out others to help them feel safe when they're stressed or afraid, and those with a fearful attachment type tend to distance themselves from others out of fear of not being worthy of taking the other person's time or attention when they need it. Both of these insecure types create a lot of internal conflict. If you scored high for both preoccupied and fearful, it means you have an internal push and pull to be close while fearing being hurt and abandoned.

Attachment conflict may be something you feel, as Tony did. He wanted his mother to love him, notice him, and appreciate him for his deeds and successes, but she only saw his mistakes and failures. His fearful attachment type left him conflicted inside, feeling a push and pull between the love he wanted and needed and the expression of love he received. This attachment type showed up in his life as conflict—his changing emphasis on grades, his inability to accept help from his coach, his strong need to be with Pam coupled with feeling unworthy of her and her attention, and his attempts to gain approval and love from his mother by trying different things to please her. His attachment type was the source of a lot of confusion, and it worsened his experience of BPD.

Have you felt like Tony did? This conflict motivates and affects how you behave, feel, and act toward yourself and others and in relationships. At the heart of it is your attachment type. Attachment is the motivator that drives us to try to connect, get close, and be vulnerable, but it also causes us to feel afraid, lonely, abandoned, and scared as a result of that same connection. But it didn't have to be this way for Tony, nor does it have to be this way for you. Attachment styles can change over time. With effort you can learn new skills to attach differently (Levy et al. 2006).

Changing Your Attachment Style

Attachment is a great motivator in our relationships and our emotional lives. When our attachment type is insecure, we have greater difficulty in many parts of our life, including with controlling our emotions and managing our relationships, but you're not stuck with this attachment type, just as you're not stuck with BPD. You can reroute the motivation of attachment to work for you, not against you.

Research shows that individuals can become more securely attached, both through changing how they see themselves and others and by encouraging new patterns of adaptive functioning (Levy et al. 2006). The change comes about when you establish new adaptive and healthy patterns by exploring and challenging your negative beliefs, behaviors, and ways of functioning, such as by examining your past (which we're doing in part 1 of this workbook), learning and using self-soothing techniques to enhance self-control, and recognizing what triggers drive you to fall into those old negative ways of dealing with yourself, others, and situations.

Now that you know a little about attachment theory, have an idea of your attachment type, and know that you can change it, take a few minutes to reflect on how you think it shows itself in your life and your relationships. Think of your attachment type as a new way of looking at some painful issues around your BPD. Be curious as you do this exercise. There are no right or wrong answers, you're just exploring.

How do you think your attachment type explains your motivations for connecting to others? How does it affect your fear of being close to others—or your fear of losing them?

_____

_____

_____

_____

How do you think your attachment type affects how you see yourself? List some words you'd use to describe yourself in relation to other people, and write a little about how those descriptions match up with your attachment style.

How do you think your attachment type affects your relationships? Reflect on a couple of your most significant and more casual relationships through the lens of your attachment type. Do you behave differently in casual relationships versus deeper ones?

Describe what push and pull you feel the most as a result of your attachment type. For example, do you feel the desire to be closer to others but are afraid to do so, so you isolate yourself?

These questions may have confused or frustrated you, leaving you unsure of what responses to put down. Or you may have started writing one thing and veered off into other territory altogether. Or the answers you came up with may have left you feeling discouraged or overwhelmed. These are all common experiences, and it's fine if any of them happened. We're just starting our exploration, and that involves looking at ourselves in new ways and seeing what we discover. Your BPD doesn't want you to explore; it wants you to stay stuck. But you recognized a need for change, to do things differently, and working to change your attachment type is a part of that journey. The process of changing your attachment type is not an easy one. If it were easy, there wouldn't be BPD workbooks, and some psychologists might be out of a job. But it is possible.

Setting the Stage for Success

Using the spaces below, pull together what you learned from this chapter so you can take this information with you.

The most helpful information I learned from this chapter:

1. _____

2. _____

3. _____

While going through this chapter, I was thinking _____, and it helped me to see that _____

_____

As you explored the roots of your BPD and your attachment type, you probably wondered if all BPD is the same. It isn't, and in the next chapter we're going to explore the four BPD subtypes and identify the subtype (or subtypes) that best reflects your experience.

CHAPTER 4

What Is Your BPD Type?

You learned a lot about BPD in the preceding chapters, including how it develops and presents itself in your life. No single process created your BPD, and as we continue to explore this disorder you'll learn there's no singular type of BPD either. In this chapter, we're going to explore the four subtypes of BPD. A *subtype* is a different presentation or form of an idea or concept. For our purposes, "borderline personality disorder" is the general term we use for this disorder, and the subtypes are the specific presentations, or forms, of BPD. In this chapter you'll also complete an assessment in which you identify the subtype (or subtypes) that best represents your BPD. Learning about your subtype will help you better understand your BPD, and the more you know the more prepared you are to grow beyond it.

The Four BPD Subtypes

There are four subtypes of BPD: discouraged, impulsive, petulant, and self-destructive (Millon 1996). Let's briefly go over each and see which subtype (or subtypes) fits you best.

Discouraged: These individuals tend to have difficulty making up their mind, have a strong need to be around others, have intense internal anger that builds until they explode, and act out when they feel "pushed" to defend themselves or when they feel they're not being heard.

Impulsive: These individuals are often flirtatious, tend to focus on the surface of things rather than going deeply into any one issue, have high energy but lose interest in things and people easily, and act without thinking. Others tend to not know what these individuals will do next.

Petulant: These individuals tend to be quick to express annoyance or dissatisfaction, have difficulty waiting their turn, are easily frustrated, and see the world as hurtful and negative. Others are uncertain about how these individuals will behave next.

Self-destructive: These individuals tend to have difficulty making decisions, may be humble in one instance and then inflexible the next, tend to be undecided about most things, behave without thinking about the consequences, may hurt themselves physically, and see themselves in a very loathsome and negative way.

As you went through this list, did you try to identify which subtype (or subtypes) fits you best? In the next section we're going to do just that—identify your subtype.

Identifying Your BPD Subtype

In the assessment below, circle how often you have the thoughts and feelings or exhibit the behaviors that are listed. Try not to overthink your responses, rather answer from your gut. Keep in mind that it's common for people to score high on more than one subtype; this means that you have tendencies that fit more than one subtype. Don't use this information to feel bad about or to attack yourself. You're only identifying the frequency of your thoughts, feelings, and behaviors. Remember, your BPD doesn't want you to explore and grow beyond it, so if doing this assessment brings up too many thoughts, feelings, and memories, take a break, talk to a mental health provider or a trusted friend, and come back to it when you're ready. You can download a copy of this assessment at http://www.newharbinger.com/42730.

Borderline Personality Disorder Subtype Assessment*

	Never 0	Rarely 1	Sometimes 2	Often 3

	0	1	2	3
1. I easily attach to others emotionally.	0	1	2	3
2. I am flirtatious to get the attention of someone else.	0	1	2	3
3. People have a hard time determining what my next move is going to be.	0	1	2	3
4. I tend to act without thinking things through.	0	1	2	3
5. It's hard for me to abide by a commitment without input from someone else.	0	1	2	3
6. I like to find exciting experiences.	0	1	2	3
7. I'm easily annoyed or made angry.	0	1	2	3
8. It's hard for me to make a decision.	0	1	2	3
9. I require someone or something else for financial or emotional support, or some other type of support.	0	1	2	3
10. I have a lot of energy.	0	1	2	3
11. I have a hard time waiting for others.	0	1	2	3
12. I tend to apologize if someone is being aggressive toward me.	0	1	2	3
13. I hold my anger inside until I explode if pressured.	0	1	2	3
14. I'm easily bored.	0	1	2	3
15. I tend not to change my attitude or opinion, especially when there are good reasons to do so.	0	1	2	3
16. I dislike myself intensely.	0	1	2	3

17. I'm likely to physically hurt myself.	0	1	2	3
18. Once I start something I cannot stop.	0	1	2	3
19. I tend to see the worst side of things or believe that the worst will happen.	0	1	2	3
20. I engage in dangerous activities, even if it means I'm likely to get hurt.	0	1	2	3

*Please remember that this is a tool to identify which subtype on the BPD spectrum (see chapter 1 for an explanation of the BPD spectrum) best fits your view and approach to the world. This is a tool to increase your insight into BPD, not to diagnose it.

Scoring Chart

Write in the value you circled for each question below the question number. For example, if you circled 3 for question 1, write a 3 under the block for question 1. Do this for all the questions. Then add up the values to determine your score for each BPD subtype. The subtype (or subtypes) that has the highest value fits you best.

Discouraged subtype	1	5	9	13	17	Total
Impulsive subtype	2	6	10	14	18	Total
Petulant subtype	3	7	11	15	19	Total
Self-destructive subtype	4	8	12	16	20	Total

Circle your BPD subtype, or subtypes, below:

Discouraged   Impulsive   Petulant   Self-destructive

Once you've determined which subtype (or subtypes) fits you best, go back to the definitions above and see how much you feel the subtype fits. Answering the following questions can help you explore your thoughts, feelings, and memories related to having identified your BPD subtype.

What do you think about yourself and your life now that you've identified your BPD subtype (or subtypes)?

_____
_____
_____
_____

How do you feel having identified your BPD subtype (or subtypes)?

_____
_____
_____
_____

To the best of your ability and to the degree you feel comfortable, describe any memories related to your BPD subtype (or subtypes).

_____
_____
_____
_____

Setting the Stage for Success

Using the spaces below, pull together what you learned from this chapter so you can take this information with you.

The most helpful information I learned from this chapter:

1. _____

2. _____

3. _____

While going through this chapter, I was thinking _____, and it helped me to see that _____

_____

_____

Now that you've identified your subtype (or subtypes), we're going to identify and explore your BPD symptoms and prognosis.

CHAPTER 5

BPD Symptoms

In this chapter we're going to explore the symptoms associated with your BPD and identify those that are most problematic for you. We'll then examine the likelihood of you overcoming BPD. This knowledge will expand your awareness of BPD and how it impacts you and your life, and it will hopefully encourage you to continue this journey of growth and self-discovery.

Identifying the Intensity of Your BPD Symptoms

Remember Betty from chapter 1? Her issues with BPD seemed unmanageable when taken as a whole, but when she and I explored her symptoms individually and then identified those that caused her the greatest amount of difficulty, she was able to focus her treatment, reduce the interference from those symptoms, and ultimately learn to control them. When you look at BPD broadly, as a whole disorder, it's overwhelming, but when you examine it at the symptom-specific level, you can identify areas to focus on. Approaching BPD in this way makes it more manageable.

Symptoms are the emotions, thoughts, and behaviors related to your BPD. The Symptom Expression Rating Form below will help you identify the symptoms that are causing you the greatest problems. Complete the form by identifying the intensity of each symptom within the last two weeks. For example, if you felt that you were reactive in an extreme way, you'd rate it a 10, but if you felt you were minimally reactive, you'd rate this symptom a 2. Do your best to rate each symptom honestly, from 0 (none) to 10 (extreme), as doing so will help you identify those symptoms that cause you the greatest difficulty. BPD symptoms change over time, so this form is available for download at http://www.newharbinger.com/42730. You may want to revisit your symptoms as you continue your journey beyond BPD.

Symptom Expression Rating Form

Symptoms	Intensity None/Mild/Moderate/ Severe/Extreme
Highly reactive	0 1 2 3 4 5 6 7 8 9 10
Tend to have intense relationships	0 1 2 3 4 5 6 7 8 9 10
Lack empathy	0 1 2 3 4 5 6 7 8 9 10
Quick to intimacy	0 1 2 3 4 5 6 7 8 9 10
Easily influenced	0 1 2 3 4 5 6 7 8 9 10
Speech lacks detail	0 1 2 3 4 5 6 7 8 9 10
Feel a strong sense of emptiness	0 1 2 3 4 5 6 7 8 9 10
Feel intense anger	0 1 2 3 4 5 6 7 8 9 10
Feel paranoid when stressed	0 1 2 3 4 5 6 7 8 9 10
Feel deserving of privileges or special treatment	0 1 2 3 4 5 6 7 8 9 10
Require constant admiration	0 1 2 3 4 5 6 7 8 9 10
Take advantage of others for own gain	0 1 2 3 4 5 6 7 8 9 10
Easily excited and display emotions as they occur	0 1 2 3 4 5 6 7 8 9 10
Feel abandoned	0 1 2 3 4 5 6 7 8 9 10
Unsure of who I am	0 1 2 3 4 5 6 7 8 9 10
Feel intense self-importance	0 1 2 3 4 5 6 7 8 9 10
Have fantasies of power	0 1 2 3 4 5 6 7 8 9 10
Impulsive	0 1 2 3 4 5 6 7 8 9 10
Tend to feel detached when under stress	0 1 2 3 4 5 6 7 8 9 10
Need to be center of attention	0 1 2 3 4 5 6 7 8 9 10

See self as totally unique	0 1 2 3 4 5 6 7 8 9 10
Gain attention via appearance	0 1 2 3 4 5 6 7 8 9 10
Have superficial emotional expression	0 1 2 3 4 5 6 7 8 9 10
Inappropriately sexually seductive or provocative	0 1 2 3 4 5 6 7 8 9 10
Engage in self-harm behavior, threats, or gestures	0 1 2 3 4 5 6 7 8 9 10

Now that you've rated the intensity of your symptoms, circle those that you rated a 7 or above. These are your primary symptoms, the ones with the greatest impact on you and those around you.

Primary Symptoms

Highly reactive	Tend to have intense relationships	Lack empathy
Quick to intimacy	Easily influenced	Speech lacks detail
Feel a strong sense of emptiness	Feel intense anger	Feel paranoid when stressed
Feel deserving of privileges or special treatment	Require constant admiration	Take advantage of others for own gain
Easily excited and display emotions as they occur	Feel abandoned	Unsure of who I am
Feel intense self-importance	Have fantasies of power	Impulsive
Tend to feel detached when under stress	Need to be center of attention	See self as totally unique
Gain attention via appearance	Have superficial emotional expression	Inappropriately sexually seductive or provocative
Engage in self-harm behavior, threats, or gestures		

When you look at the primary symptoms you circled, how do you feel about yourself and your BPD?

_____
_____
_____
_____

Can you identify the situations and memories that encourage these primary symptoms?

What can you say to yourself so you don't use this information to attack yourself and encourage your BPD?

_____

_____

_____

_____

Betty completed the same symptoms expression form and identified her primary symptoms.

Betty's Primary Symptoms

Highly reactive	Tend to have intense relationships	Lack empathy
Quick to intimacy	Easily influenced	Speech lacks detail
Feel a strong sense of emptiness	Feel intense anger	Feel paranoid when stressed
Feel deserving of privileges or special treatment	Require constant admiration	Take advantage of others for own gain
Easily excited and display emotions as they occur	Feel abandoned	Unsure of who I am
Feel intense self-importance	Have fantasies of power	Impulsive
Tend to feel detached when under stress	Need to be center of attention	See self as totally unique
Gain attention via appearance	Have superficial emotional expression	Inappropriately sexually seductive or provocative
Engage in self-harm behavior, threats, or gestures		

Now that you've identified your primary symptoms, answer the following questions to increase your awareness of the thoughts, feelings, and memories related to this exploration.

Describe how seeing Betty's rating form, and comparing it to yours, makes you feel.

_____

_____

_____

_____

What do you think about Betty, having seen her primary symptoms?

_____

_____

_____

_____

Avoid the tendency to self-attack. It's not uncommon to feel like you marked the most symptoms ever in the history of the world. This judgment is a form of self-attack that most people with BPD engage in, but it's false. Remember, don't use these symptoms to judge yourself. Choose instead to tell yourself that these are just your BPD symptoms, and remind yourself that you're using this knowledge to do it differently in the future. I listed Betty's responses so that you'd see that other people circle lots of symptoms on this form. Even if you circled more symptoms than Betty, it doesn't mean you're hopeless or a lost cause. As you move through this workbook, you'll learn to counter such false beliefs and reduce your symptoms and replace them with accurate assessments of who you are as you grow beyond your BPD and develop adaptive and healthy response patterns.

Prognosis: Will I Get Better or Worse?

The term *prognosis* refers to the way something, such as a disease, a disorder, or an ailment, progresses or develops. In this workbook, I use the term in the sense of the likelihood of one overcoming or growing beyond BPD. A *good prognosis* means one is likely to reduce the severity of symptoms, or overcome BPD altogether, and a *poor prognosis* means that the individual is unlikely to experience reduced symptoms or to overcome BPD.

You're probably wondering what your prognosis is. The following may help you see it more clearly. Many people don't know that folks who have BPD tend to seek treatment. Research shows that 88 percent of individuals with BPD stay in treatment and that recovery is possible (Zanarini et al. 2010). Just the fact that you picked up this book is a good sign. Perhaps you're also participating in group or individual therapy, or both. Research has shown that people diagnosed with BPD tend to improve over time; a study found that 50 percent of individuals with BPD recovered, defined as a remission of symptoms and having good cognitive, emotional, social, and vocational functioning (Battle et al. 2004; Zanarini et al. 2005; Zanarini et al. 2016). So please take heart; BPD is not like a tattoo you're stuck with for the rest of your life, but something that you can control and grow beyond by building your awareness and using the right tools.

Take a moment to reflect on your own prognosis by answering the following questions.

Circle the prognosis you'd give yourself today regarding your BPD?

GOOD   POOR

What supports this prognosis? Think of what you've learned in this workbook so far, or of experiences you've had in life.

_____

_____

_____

_____

Setting the Stage for Success

Using the spaces below, pull together what you learned from this chapter so you can take this information with you.

The most helpful information I learned from this chapter:

1. _____

2. _____

3. _____

While going through this chapter, I was thinking _____, and it helped me to see that _____

_____

_____

You made it to the end of part 1 of the workbook! This is a great accomplishment. Developing knowledge, awareness, and skills is the starting point of your journey to overcome BPD. To help strengthen what you've learned, there's a summary available for download at http://www.newharbinger. com/42730. This summary pulls together the concepts, activities, and exercises from part 1 of the workbook, so I highly recommend that you take the time to go through it before moving on to part 2.

In part 2 of the workbook we're going to focus on addressing and changing the problematic beliefs, behaviors, and patterns that affect how you see yourself, feel about yourself, and interact with others in various situations.

PART 2

First Steps for Growing Beyond BPD

CHAPTER 6

Where You Are in the Process of Change

In this chapter I'll introduce you to the stages of change and explain how they relate to your BPD. I included an evaluation for you to complete, which will help you determine where you are within the stages of change, as well as questions to help you move forward.

The Stages of Change

The change process is unique for each of us in many ways, but it also follows a series of somewhat universal stages, including precontemplation, contemplation, preparation, action, maintenance, and relapse (Prochaska, DiClemente, and Norcross 1992; Prochaska, Norcross, and DiClemente 2013). We'll use these stages to identify and evaluate where you are in your change process and to prepare you to move forward and overcome your BPD.

As Betty began to think about the stages of change, she felt uncertain. She weighed her options: taking the evaluation, knowing where she was in the process of change, and helping herself and those she knew and loved versus staying in difficult relationships, having trouble with employment, and feeling lost and empty inside. Betty had normal fears and concerns about the evaluation, and you may have some of your own. The process of change is scary for many people, and you're probably comfortable with your BPD—to a degree. Betty certainly was. BPD can seem like an old pillow, but one with thorns; you've had it so long that you're comfortable with it even though it hurts you. The pain you know probably feels safer than the comfort and safety you don't yet know.

But growing beyond your BPD and using adaptive and healthy response patterns to manage situations, relationships, and stress is a good thing. Having more control over your life is a powerful thing. That's why we're going to examine where you are within the stages of change. Knowing where you're at will challenge you to move into the other stages, and it will increase your readiness to continue to tackle your BPD. In the end, Betty chose to evaluate where she was, and eventually she was glad she did.

Stages of Change Evaluation

For each statement below, write a checkmark in the column (true or false) that reflects how you feel today. There are no right or wrong answers. Please answer all questions to the best of your ability.

Stages of Change Statements	True	False
1. I have issues in my life that I need to work on.		
2. I am making changes in my life.		
3. I don't see any problems with my life right now.		
4. I know I need better resources to help me stop myself from going back to my old, unhealthy behaviors.		
5. I am ready to do things differently.		
6. I need a little help to continue doing things differently.		
7. Everyone else is the problem, not me.		
8. I am working to prevent myself from relapsing back to my old, unhealthy behaviors.		
9. I think it's time to do things differently.		
10. There's really nothing I need to change about me or how I'm living my life.		
11. I want to learn more about how my life would change if I did things differently.		
12. Anyone can talk about change, but I am doing it.		
13. I'm not sure what will cause me to fall back into my old, unhealthy behaviors.		
14. I'm not sure I am ready to do things differently in my life.		
15. I am working to overcome obstacles in order to change my life.		
16. I'm ready to put things in place to make a change.		

17. I am aware of and encourage my new healthy behaviors and seek support when necessary.		
18. I had some success doing things differently but fell back into my old ways of doing things.		

Now score yourself. True answers are 1 point and false answers are 0 points. Write the points for each statement in the scoring sheet below. For example, to determine your precontemplation score you'd total the points for questions 3, 7, and 10.

Precontemplation	3. _____	
	7. _____	
	10. _____	Total: _____
Contemplation	1. _____	
	9. _____	
	14. _____	Total: _____
Preparation	5. _____	
	11. _____	
	16. _____	Total: _____
Action	2. _____	
	12. _____	
	15. _____	Total: _____
Maintenance	6. _____	
	8. _____	
	17. _____	Total: _____
Relapse	4. _____	
	13. _____	
	18. _____	Total: _____

You may find that you have two stages with the same score. This indicates that you're within or between these two stages, and that's okay. Betty scored highest in the preparation stage. She had tried a few things in the past, had picked up a workbook because she knew she needed to learn and then practice skills to grow beyond her BPD, and felt ready to move forward. With her results she prepared to move into the action phase. Now that you know where you're at in the stages of change, let's look at each stage.

Precontemplation

At this stage you're not considering changing anytime soon. You're unaware that a problem exists, but family, friends, and coworkers are aware that there's a problem. If you seek help at this stage in the process it's due to pressure from others.

If you rated this stage of change the highest, what thoughts and feelings do you have about changing?

_____
_____
_____
_____

What are you uncertain about when you think about changing?

_____

What would it take to make you start thinking about addressing and changing your problem?

_____
_____
_____
_____

Contemplation

At this stage you're aware that problems exist but remain uncertain if you want to change or what's involved with changing. You may be weighing your options: should you stay where you are or invest effort in doing things differently. You may have purchased this workbook because you're thinking about doing things differently and you want to know what's involved in the process.

If you rated this stage of change the highest, what's keeping you from changing?

_____
_____
_____

Do you see benefits for staying where you are with the problems and issues you have related to BPD? What are the benefits?

_____

_____

_____

_____

What might you gain by changing your negative beliefs, behaviors, and patterns?

_____

_____

_____

Preparation

In this stage you're testing the waters of change. You've committed to doing things differently and are getting ready to challenge your BPD symptoms and address issues. This may be why you're going through this workbook. You may have developed a plan or a timeline for incorporating the exercises, techniques, and worksheets of this workbook into your schedule.

If you rated this stage of change the highest, what areas of your BPD do you want to be sure to address and overcome?

_____

_____

_____

Who can you consult for social support as you begin this journey of change?

_____

_____

As you prepare for action, what obstacles may be in your way and how can you minimize their interference?

_____

_____

_____

Action

In this stage you're engaged and ready to challenge, control, and defeat those negative beliefs, behaviors, and response patterns related to BPD. You'll go through the workbook and use the skills you learn, incorporating them into your views of self and others and the situations you're in. You're committing time and effort to change and growth. At times during this process of change you may feel a sense of loss for the old negative beliefs, behaviors, and response patterns that you're leaving behind. Remember that this is a normal reaction, and you should continue to commit yourself to the process of defeating your BPD.

If you rated this stage of change the highest, what particular BPD issues do you want to change first?

_____

_____

_____

What can you do to empower yourself to get around barriers to your growth?

_____

_____

_____

What can you do to remind yourself of the long-term benefits of adaptive and healthy change?

_____

_____

_____

Maintenance

By this stage you've made the changes you need to make to develop adaptive and healthy response patterns, behaviors, thoughts, and skills for self-control. You're committed to adaptive and healthy functioning.

If you rated this stage of change the highest, what can you do to remind yourself about the gains you've made and the successes you've had?

_____

_____

_____

Who can you keep in your life who will help you remain on this course of adaptive and healthy functioning?

What can you do to prevent yourself from sliding back into old beliefs, behaviors, and patterns?

Relapse

It's natural to slide back into old habits. It might happen while addressing significant triggers (drugs, alcohol, and difficult relationships) or when encountering new barriers to change. You may not relapse, but it's a stage of change because everyone has a unique change process and encounters very individual situations. The most important point about relapse is this:

Relapse may be part of your process, but so is reengagement.

A research study found that of those who relapse, 15 percent fall back to the precontemplation stage but 85 percent go back to the contemplation stage (Prochaska, Norcross, and DiClemente 2013). What this means is that the majority of people who relapse into old negative beliefs, behaviors, and patterns go back to thinking about changing and then reenter the change process. If you relapse while tackling your BPD, have faith that this is okay and expected. Eventually you'll resume the process of change and can and will do things differently and better in the future.

If you rated this stage of change the highest, what triggers and barriers do you think caused you to relapse?

_____

_____

_____

What has helped you control your triggers and overcome barriers?

_____

_____

_____

Can you identify a mantra, quote, or saying that motivates you to change? If so, put it in your phone, on your fridge at home, or anywhere you'll see it regularly.

The stages of change and the process of moving through them are fluid. Change doesn't really remain still but flows like water in a river. Your growth will be a fluid process, and because of that you should feel free to return to the preceding evaluation as many times as you like as you go through this workbook in order to assess where you are in the process of change. It's available for download at http://www.newharbinger.com/42730.

Solidifying Steps to Growth

Using the spaces below, pull together what you learned from this chapter so you can take this information with you.

The most helpful information I learned from this chapter:

1. _____
2. _____
3. _____

The skills that I want to practice:

1. _____
2. _____
3. _____

While going through this chapter, I was thinking _____, and it helped me to see that _____
_____
_____

Next we'll explore the negative beliefs, behaviors, and benefits that have kept your BPD in place for so long.

CHAPTER 7

Beliefs, Behaviors, and Benefits That Keep You Stuck

This chapter is going to help you identify the beliefs that drive your behaviors, and how both come together to form negative response patterns. We'll also examine the short-lived benefits that keep your negative response patterns active and in place. These benefits are the real goals behind negative behaviors, but they come with long-term costs. Learning about these negative response patterns and figuring out how to control them are major steps toward empowering yourself and growing beyond your BPD, making it more likely that you'll get both the short-term and long-term benefits you want and need more often.

From Beliefs to Benefits

We wouldn't have negative beliefs, behaviors, and patterns if we didn't benefit from them, such as by feeling safe, heard, understood, loved, appreciated, respected, and so on. Just because you receive benefits doesn't mean that they're good, healthy, or adaptive for you.

Tony wanted his mother to love, value, and recognize him. He engaged in countless behaviors, such as doing well in school and participating in sports, trying to find something inside or outside of himself that his mother would notice, but nothing worked. He also tried to get this affection from Pam, but his beliefs about his need for love and his low self-worth caused problems in this relationship. He initiated behaviors that caused her to pull away and call him "clingy," which caused him to act in desperate ways to try and keep the relationship going. His behavior resulted in the exact opposite of what he wanted and felt he needed.

Tony's beliefs drove him to engage in behaviors to try to get some sense of being seen, heard, and loved. His behaviors seemed like automatic responses, and he felt like he had little control over what kept happening. For example, he met Meg shortly after his relationship with Pam ended, and the cycle repeated itself. He had the same negative beliefs and engaged in the same behaviors with her. Of course, this negative response pattern had originated with his mother. Even though this pattern would end with him losing his objects of love, he did receive short-lived benefits. Both Pam and Meg made him feel seen, heard, and loved, and they both offered physical affection and verbal acknowledgment (that is, "I miss you too," "I think you're special too")—until they broke up with him.

In order for Tony to change his negative response patterns, he had to explore the beliefs that prompted his behaviors and came together to form his pattern, from which he reaped the short-term benefits that caused this cycle to continue—over and over again. You probably have a pattern yourself, so let's see if we can identify it. To do this, we need to start by uncovering your beliefs.

Beliefs

A *belief* is an idea or principle that we judge to be true. Beliefs develop over time from experiences, thoughts, feelings, and memories. You may believe that a Ferrari is a fast car or that all people are untrustworthy, and they may be the result of you having seen a Ferrari in a race or of having people in your life who have betrayed your trust. You have beliefs about all aspects of life, including how you see yourself, others, your past, your present, and your future, and they are directly related to your BPD. To change your BPD, you have to explore what impacts how you see and interpret life, and your beliefs are a big part of that. To help develop your awareness of your beliefs, please finish the prompts below. Don't hold back or evaluate your responses. Just write your true beliefs.

I believe I am ... _____
_____
_____

I believe others are ... _____
_____
_____

I believe my past is ... _____
_____

I believe my present is ... _____
_____

I believe my future is ... _____
_____

Describing your beliefs will help you understand how you see the world and yourself in it. Your BPD doesn't want you to do this; it prefers you to have unexplored beliefs. They cause you confusion and uncertainty, which drive you to engage in the negative response patterns that keep you connected to BPD. You've taken the first step—identifying your beliefs—so now let's go a little deeper by exploring your behaviors and patterns.

Behaviors

Behaviors are the activities we engage in that are motivated by our beliefs, and your BPD beliefs tend to drive unhealthy reoccurring behaviors. Take some time to identify the behaviors that are responses to the beliefs you have about yourself, others, the past, the present, or the future, which you listed in the preceding exercise. You can download a blank copy of this exercise at http://www.ne wharbinger.com/42730, so you can explore each belief you identified above and its influence on your behavior as much as you like. The more you do this, the greater your awareness will become.

I believe I am _____, which leads me to (write about your behavior in as much detail as you can) ... _____

_____

_____

I believe others are _____, which leads me to (write about your behavior in as much detail as you can) ... _____

I believe my past is _____, which leads me to (write about your behavior in as much detail as you can) ... _____

I believe my present is _____, which leads me to (write about your behavior in as much detail as you can) ... _____

I believe my future is _____, which leads me to (write about your behavior in as much detail as you can) ... _____

Doing this exercise can reveal the influence that your beliefs have on your behaviors. When unhealthy beliefs and behaviors come together, they create negative response patterns. These patterns are what cause continual problems, as they tend to be hurtful—both for yourself and those around you

Negative Response Patterns

Patterns are groups of behaviors, and over time they become your default automatic responses to beliefs, other people, and situations. Patterns are created when you have experiences, thoughts, feelings, or memories that cause beliefs, which drive behaviors. Because they tend to be automatic, you may not be aware that you're engaging in a pattern until you're dealing with short-term and long-term consequences. It would be difficult and tiresome to go through the steps of identifying the behind-the-scenes beliefs and behaviors every time you engage in a negative response pattern, so you're going to name your pattern in the exercise below so you can quickly recognize it.

Before we get to the exercise, let's take a look at the belief and behaviors that make up one of Tony's patterns (figure 3). Tony identified that his belief "I'm not important enough to be loved" drove him to call Pam continually, as well as engage in other behaviors, to see if she cared about him. He named this pattern "See how much I love you so you'll love me."

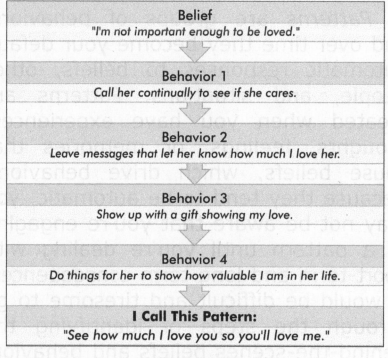

Figure 3

To control and change his pattern, Tony needed to be aware of what he was thinking and doing. Now it's your turn to identify what makes up your patterns. In this workbook, we're only going to identify one pattern, but most people have several patterns they fall into each and every day, and the more patterns you identify the more aware you'll become of what fuels your BPD. You can download this worksheet, Identifying Negative Response Patterns, at http://www.newharbinger.com/4273 0, so you can identify more patterns. I encourage you to do this. Take your time putting all the pieces of your pattern together. Don't worry about the name. You can name the pattern anything you want, because the name is just for you. The name is usually very personal.

Identifying Negative Response Patterns

Belief

Behavior 1

Behavior 2

Behavior 3

Behavior 4

I Call This Pattern:

We all use patterns to try to get benefits out of them. Some patterns are adaptive and healthy, and some are harmful and hurtful, and this can determine the type of benefit we get from them. Individuals with BPD tend to have default patterns that are harmful, that keep BPD present, and keep you feeling stuck with your BPD due to pull of the short-term benefits. To grow beyond your patterns and your BPD, you have to recognize the benefits that cause you to keep using your negative response patterns.

Benefits

You may be reluctant to identify the benefits you get from your negative response patterns because you're afraid of losing the benefits. But in order to grow beyond these patterns and to develop more adaptive and healthy ways to receive the benefits you desire, it's crucial to do so.

Tony identified three benefits from his negative response pattern "See how much I love you so you'll love me" (see figure 5). These were the strong short-term benefits for him that came with long-term consequences—that is, he alienated those he cared for. This cycle repeated itself, leaving him feeling unfulfilled, alone, worthless, and invisible.

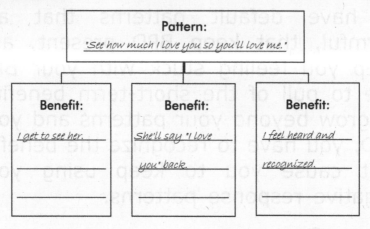

Pattern:
"See how much I love you so you'll love me."

Benefit:
I get to see her.

Benefit:
She'll say "I love you" back.

Benefit:
I feel heard and recognized.

Long-Term Consequences:
She feels suffocated and overwhelmed and breaks up with me, leaving me feeling worthless, invisible, and unable to find someone who cares about me, which drives me to find someone as fast as I can and to drink a lot.

Figure 5

Now that you've seen Tony's short-term benefits and long-term consequences from one of his patterns, it's your turn to identify the benefits and consequences of one of your patterns. Be as honest as you can, and remember that the goal is to understand what drives you to fall back into negative beliefs, behaviors, and patterns. You can download this worksheet, Identifying Short-Term Benefits, at http://www.newharbinger.com/42730 and perform this exercise for all of the patterns you identify.

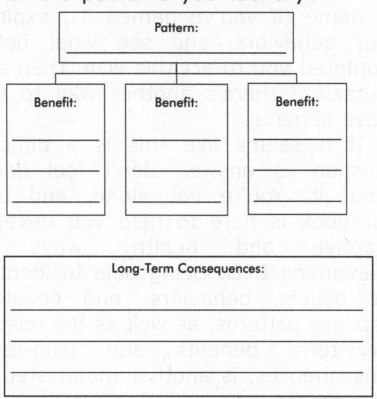

Pattern:

Benefit:

Benefit:

Benefit:

Long-Term Consequences:

Now that you see how beliefs, behaviors, negative response patterns, and benefits interact with each other, can you see why your negative response patterns remain in place? Do you have a better understanding of the long-term consequences you have to deal with? The next time you find yourself in a situation in which you're trying to get some benefits, stop and work backward through the process we discussed in this chapter: acknowledge your pattern by name (if you've named it), explore your behaviors, and see what belief prompted you to act this way. Then ask yourself if there's another way to get these benefits.

If it seems like this is a difficult question to answer, don't feel down about it. You're not alone, and this workbook is here to help you develop adaptive and healthy ways of overcoming BPD. Being able to identify the beliefs, behaviors, and negative response patterns, as well as the related short-term benefits and long-term consequences, is another major step in the process.

Solidifying Steps to Growth

Using the spaces below, pull together what you learned from this chapter so you can take this information with you.

The most helpful information I learned from this chapter:

1. _____
2. _____
3. _____

The skills that I want to practice:

1. _____
2. _____
3. _____

While going through this chapter, I was thinking _____, and it helped me to see that _____

_____

_____

In the next chapter you're going to identify triggers—stimuli inside and outside of yourself and in the world—that impact your behavior and beliefs the most, and learn skills to manage them so they influence you less.

CHAPTER 8

The Eight Trigger Categories

In this chapter we're going to go over the eight trigger categories and help you identify which ones impact you the most. We'll then explore your triggers and go over techniques to help you manage them.

What Are Triggers?

A *trigger* is a person, situation, event, feeling, thought, or memory that leads to an internal or external response. Triggers cause a strong emotional reaction and compel us to immediately engage in default response patterns. Triggers can be connected to any of our five senses—sight, sound, taste, touch, and hearing—and were created by past experiences. Individuals with BPD are often strongly connected to their triggers and feel compelled to respond to them using their negative beliefs, behaviors, and patterns to reduce intense emotions and to get short-term benefits. (We examined these subjects in the previous chapter.) Triggers can set off a chain reaction of destruction when they're not recognized and managed.

Let's personalize these definitions by looking at a couple of Betty's triggers—feeling lonely and feeling abandoned. When she was emotionally triggered in these ways, she engaged in self-harm behaviors, such as cutting herself or promiscuity. She did these things without thinking because she felt that she must respond to her triggers immediately to reduce the stress, anxiety, fear, anger, desolation, and emptiness she felt and believed would last forever.

Does any of this sound familiar? When you're triggered it may feel like you must respond to your triggers immediately, to feel less overwhelmed and to reduce your discomfort at any cost. The great thing about triggers is that they're learned, and if they're learned that means we can change how we respond to them in order to be more adaptive. To be able to identify one's triggers it helps to understand what kinds of triggers there are.

Triggers are everywhere, and they influence how we react inwardly (toward ourselves) and outwardly (toward others). They all fall into one of eight categories. For example, we explored beliefs in chapter 7, a trigger that falls under the "thoughts and memories" category. For each trigger category in the chart below, place a checkmark in the box that feels most appropriate for you.

Is a Trigger	Is NOT a Trigger	Trigger Category	Definition
		Emotional state	Emotions, such as depression, anxiety, anger, fear, or embarrassment
		Physical state	Physical sensations, such as restlessness, boredom, tiredness, hunger
		Presence of others	People in your life who are bad or good influences
		Availability	Means to engage in destructive behavior; for example, having drugs or alcohol in the house, razors to cut yourself with, and so on
		Physical setting	Places, such as home, work, school, or parties
		Social pressure	People or friends around you who use drugs, engage in self-harm behaviors, dare or tempt you to do hurtful things, and so forth
		Activities	Things you have to do, such as running errands, working out, work or school responsibilities
		Thoughts and memories	Recollection of past experiences, beliefs, flashbacks, catastrophizing, mind reading, "shoulds and musts," black-and-white thinking, and so forth

Exploring Your Trigger Categories

Now that you've identified the categories of triggers that affect you, let's explore them further. As you're answering the following questions, be aware of the thoughts, feelings, and memories that are connected to the trigger categories. Try not to hold back;

let it all out. If you feel overwhelmed, take a break, talk to a positive friend or mental health provider, and, when you feel ready to reengage, come back to the exercise.

What is the origin or root of the trigger categories you identified?

_____

_____

_____

_____

What people, places, and things fit into the trigger categories you identified?

_____

_____

_____

_____

Why do you think one or more of the trigger categories *do not* impact you?

_____

_____

_____

What behaviors do you tend to engage in when you're triggered?

List two or three behaviors you can engage in when you're triggered instead of your default, or immediate, responses?

Many individuals with BPD tend not to explore their triggers, which empowers their BPD. Having done this exercise, in which you explored your trigger categories, you've weakened your BPD and empowered yourself to grow beyond it. Now it's time to gain control over your triggers.

Managing Your Triggers

Whether your triggers are internal, external, or both, *you* can control them. The first part of this chapter was designed to raise your awareness of the trigger categories that impact you most. Now you're going to use that information to understand them, yourself, and the world around you. Circle how much control you feel you have over your internal and external triggers, and then answer the questions that follow.

0	1	2	3	4	5
None	Very little	Little	Some	A lot	Complete

What about yourself, others, and the world did you consider when circling your answer?

_____
_____
_____

What prevents you from having more control over your triggers?

_____
_____
_____

What would give you more control over your triggers?

_____
_____
_____

Enhancing your control over your triggers is one component of managing and growing beyond your BPD, and the helpful and healthy response techniques below are to help you manage how you want to respond when you're triggered.

Mindfulness

Mindfulness is a technique designed to help you calmly focus your awareness on your bodily sensations, thoughts, and feelings. Mindfulness will help you lessen or eliminate that drive to respond when you're triggered. The very first step in our exercise is to find an object that has value to you. It can be a smooth or rough rock; a stuffed animal; a special pen, pencil, or crayon; a fidget spinner—anything you want. Once you have your object, follow these steps:

1. Grab your object.
2. Feel it. Is it rough, smooth, soft, or some other texture?
3. Focus your attention on the object, and only the object. Let words, thoughts, and feelings float out of your head, as if they're attached to a hot-air balloon.

4.   Stay present without reacting to your words, thoughts, and feelings.
5.   Imagine one of your triggers and focus on the words, thoughts, and feelings that come up, but don't react.
6.   Imagine a response, other than your default response, that is positive, helpful, and encouraging.
7.   Engage in this alternate response.

"Let It Out" List

The "let it out" list is a wonderful technique for releasing the energy from your trigger in a positive, nondestructive way. It entails making a list of all the things you're thinking and feeling when you get triggered. Once you've expressed your negative response energy, you're in a better place to manage what triggered you. You can keep your list on your phone, on your computer, or anywhere that's useful for when you're triggered.

1.   Go to a place that's private and away from others (for example, your car or another room).

2. Open an app on your phone or computer or use a piece of paper to start your "let it out" list.

3. Write or dictate everything that comes to mind related to your trigger.

4. Don't edit your list. Don't worry about spelling, grammar, or tense. Just let it out!

5. Put everything on the list. Let all your words, thoughts, and feelings flow.

6. Do this until you've exhausted your words, thoughts, and feelings about your trigger.

7. Imagine another response, other than your default response, that is positive, helpful, and encouraging.

8. Engage in this alternate response.

The key to growing beyond BPD is to practice such skills on a routine basis. Think of a football team. Players practice all week long to master skills so they're ready for the big game on Sunday. Through practice they master skills so they'll be available when they need them. You need to do the same to grow beyond your BPD. Just as it takes a lot of exposure to the same situations and people for your triggers to develop, propelling you to respond, you need a lot of exposure to these new and healthy skills to master them. If you practice them regularly, you'll be ready when you need them most—when it's game time.

Solidifying Steps to Growth

Using the spaces below, pull together what you learned from this chapter so you can take this information with you.

The most helpful information I learned from this chapter:

1. _____

2. _____

3. _____

The skills that I want to practice:

1. _____

2. _____

3. _____

While going through this chapter, I was thinking _____, and it helped me to see that _____

In the next chapter we're going to examine positive and negative relationships, which are often intense triggers for people with BPD.

CHAPTER 9

Recognizing Positive and Negative Relationships

Relationships are difficult to maneuver through and control. Although they are important to us, we sometimes have a hard time distinguishing between the positive ones and the negative ones. What do you think about the various relationships in your life? Do you classify them as positive or negative? Most of us think about them this way, but we never go beyond that, instead choosing to remain in negative relationships that are unhealthy and overlooking or not fully engaging in the positive ones.

In this chapter you'll identify the people you're closest to, whether your relationships are negative or positive, and what makes them that way. We'll also look at the shades of gray in relationships and determine where yours fall on a relationship scale. It's hard to look at relationships to determine if they keep you stuck in negative feelings, beliefs, and BPD, but building your skill at identifying the positive and negative people and relationships in your life is an important part of growing beyond your BPD.

Exploring Relationships

In this exercise we're going to explore your negative and positive relationships, looking at how close you are to each person, the impact he or she has on you, and the degree to which you feel connected to that person. You can download a blank copy of each worksheet at http://www.newh arbinger.com/42730. Don't overthink these worksheets or worry about leaving someone off one, because you can do this exercise as often as you like. You can add as many people as you want at each level. Try to avoid having the same person on both the Negative and Unhealthy Relationships and Positive and Healthy Relationships worksheets, because you're trying to identify who falls into one or the other category to get a clearer view of how this individual impacts your life. If you have difficulty determining where to place a person, ask yourself where this person falls *most* of the time? Is he or she more often a negative or a positive influence?

Let's start by identifying how close you feel to certain people using the People in My Life worksheet. People at this level know you very well and know a lot about you and have had a lot of experiences with you. For example, you can place a child, parent, caregiver, loved one, or significant other at the first level. These people are connected to you in a very personal way, such as in a sexual or familial way or through a long-standing friendship. Tony listed Meg (his girlfriend at the time) at this first level because of how close he felt to her.

The second level can be people you work with or close friends you spend a lot of time with and who have a direct impact on you and your life. Tony listed his baseball coach at this level because he saw him regularly and felt he could talk to him about personal issues. At the third level you may place someone whom you see periodically and may have conversations with but you don't go into great detail about your personal life and feelings. People at this level are acquaintances you don't spend a lot of time with. Tony listed John, a friend of his from the baseball team whom he only saw during practice and games.

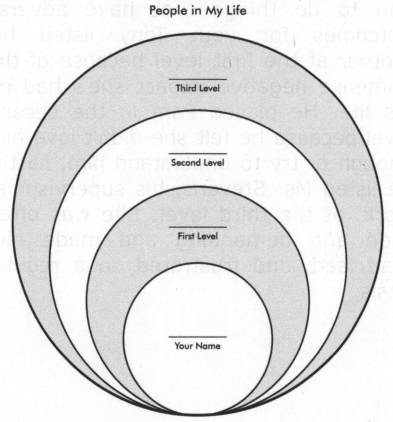

People in My Life

Third Level

Second Level

First Level

Your Name

Now, let's move on and identify your negative and unhealthy relationships.

You can include people from the People in My Life worksheet or add different people. The three levels of closeness are the same for this worksheet, but you're looking for individuals who pressure you to engage in behavior that creates regret and remorse. These are people who bring forth feelings of resentment, anger, and rage that lead you to do things that have adverse outcomes for you. Tony listed his mother at the first level because of the immense negative impact she's had on his life. He placed Pam in the second level because he felt she didn't love him enough or try to understand him. Lastly, he listed Ms. Stevens, his supervisor at work, at the third level. She was often rude and demanding and made him mad, sad, and frustrated on a regular basis.

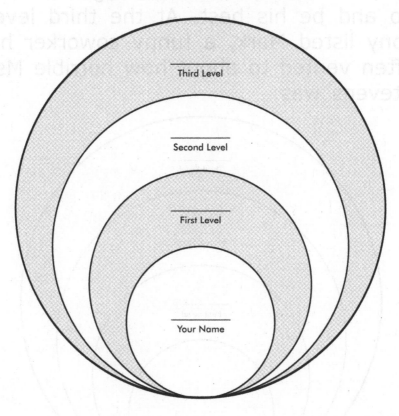

Negative and Unhealthy Relationships

Third Level

Second Level

First Level

Your Name

Next, let's identify your healthy and positive relationships. The individuals you include on this worksheet should instill in you a sense of hope, pride, and self-respect. These people encourage you to do things that are good for you and help you reach for your dreams. Tony listed Meg at the first level because he was in a close romantic relationship with her and was in love. At the second level was his baseball coach, who encouraged him to do and be his best. At the third level Tony listed Mark, a funny coworker he often vented to about how horrible Ms. Stevens was.

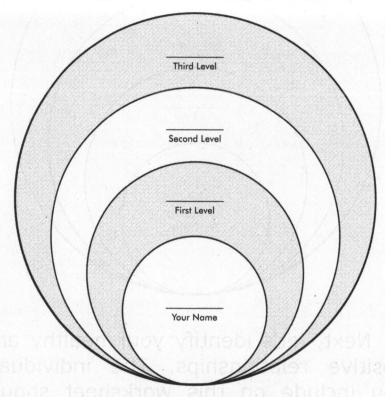

Third Level

Second Level

First Level

Your Name

Positive and Healthy Relationships

As you went through this exercise, did you find that some people were harder to classify than others? This is not uncommon, especially for individuals with BPD, and that's why going through this process is so important. Now that you've identified the degree of closeness for the people in your life, let's explore the factors that make your relationships positive or negative.

Relationship Factors

When we look at our relationships and determine if they're negative or positive, we need to identify what makes them that way. Ask yourself, *What makes my relationships negative or positive?* The answer has to do with *relationship factors,* those issues and circumstances that are unique to you and the other person, as well as the connections the two of you create. As you read through the following list of relationship factors, think about the characteristics that make the relationships you listed in the preceding exercise negative and unhealthy or positive and healthy.

Positive Relationship Factors	Negative Relationship Factors
1. We know each other very well.	1. I know little about her.
2. We can joke and be playful with each other.	2. Our relationship tends to be very serious and tense.
3. I respect his ideas.	3. He calls me names.
4. She respects my ideas.	4. She degrades me in front of others and when we're alone.
5. When we disagree, we're respectful of each other.	5. I resent him.
6. I have good memories and thoughts of him when we're not together.	6. I have fantasized about her dying or being hurt.
7. I trust her.	7. He seems to get satisfaction from my failures and difficulties.
8. I believe he has my best interests at heart.	8. She says more negative things about me than positive things.
9. She is proud and happy when things go well for me.	9. I get satisfaction kicking him when he's struggling, or at times of weakness.
10. We tend to say more positive things to each other than negative.	10. I think she's stupid.
11. I know his dreams and wishes and he knows mine.	11. I don't feel physically safe with him.
12. I'm comfortable being vulnerable in front of her.	12. I don't feel emotionally safe with her.
13. I'm able to express my true feelings in front of him.	13. I hide my true emotions from him.
14. We do not call each other names when we argue.	14. When we argue, we call each other names to hurt each other.
15. I encourage her to pursue her dreams and to succeed.	15. I have hit her.
16. I do not roll my eyes, swear at him, or call him names.	16. She has hit me.
17. We work well together under stressful situations.	17. He has embarrassed me.
18. We come together when we're stressed.	18. We make things worse when we're stressed.
19. I know her positive qualities.	19. I see her as a dumping ground for my negative emotions.
20. I can name some positive qualities I see or would want to see in our children.	20. He sees me as a dumping ground for his negative emotions.
21. He makes me feel confident about myself.	21. She has more negative than positive qualities.
22. We have fun when we're together.	22. I feel more insecure about myself when I am with him.
23. She's passionate and caring when we're together.	23. When we're intimate, I just want it to be over.
24. He can be vulnerable in front of me.	24. I resent her.
25. I feel that she appreciates me.	25. I feel like she hates me.
26. I feel that he admires me.	26. I don't trust him.
27. I feel like we're on the same team.	27. He has stolen from me.
28. She's compassionate and understanding about my past.	28. She has caused more problems in my life.
29. I believe he can get over his troubles and problems.	29. I feel like we have opposite goals in life.
30. I believe she really wants to help me get better and to succeed.	30. I do not enjoy spending time with him.
31. I enjoy spending time with him.	31. I believe she's a failure.
32. I believe she enjoys spending time with me.	32. He shows me little to no compassion or concern.
33. I know what makes him happy.	33. I would rather spend time with someone else.
34. She knows what makes me happy.	34. I feel like I spend time with her because I have to.
35. I want him to be happy.	35. I don't care if he's happy.
36. She's a source of support for me when I feel like I'm breaking down.	36. I don't feel supported or encouraged by her.
37. I feel like he pays attention to me.	37. He pays little to no attention to me.
38. I believe I am important to her.	38. I feel abused by her.
39. When we're intimate, I feel connected to him.	39. I wish he would just go away.
40. I can see a healthy future with her.	40. I see an unhealthy future with her.

Now it's your turn to identify relationship factors that play a role in some of your relationships. In the following exercise, write the name of someone from one of your relationship circles and identify the relationship factors that cause it to be positive or negative. In this exercise you're considering both sides, the positive and negative, so you can see what makes the relationship unhealthy or healthy for you. Unhealthy relationships are often what encourage the negative beliefs, behaviors, and patterns that fuel your BPD, whereas healthy relationships discourage them. You can download a blank copy of this worksheet in the summary for part 2 at http://www.new harbinger.com/42730, so you can do this exercise for as many relationships as you like.

The Positives and Negatives in My Relationship

Name: _____

Positive Relationship Factors

1. _____
2. _____
3. _____
4. _____
5. _____
6. _____

Negative Relationship Factors

1. _____
2. _____
3. _____
4. _____
5. _____
6. _____

Name: _____

Positive Relationship Factors

1. _____
2. _____
3. _____
4. _____
5. _____
6. _____

Negative Relationship Factors

1. _____
2. _____
3. _____
4. _____
5. _____
6. _____

Name: _____

Positive Relationship Factors	Negative Relationship Factors
1. _____	1. _____
2. _____	2. _____
3. _____	3. _____
4. _____	4. _____
5. _____	5. _____
6. _____	6. _____

Now that you have a better grasp of your negative and positive relationships and their relationship factors, the last step is to determine where each relationship falls on the relationship scale.

Classifying Relationships

Positive relationships are empowering, supportive, caring, and trusting. They make you feel secure with who you are. Negative relationships leave you feeling alone, hurt, uncertain, confused, and bad about yourself. Individuals with BPD tend to have more negative relationships than positive ones, and as you grow out of your BPD you'll learn how to cultivate and benefit from positive relationships.

However, determining what's positive and what's negative is tricky, because relationships are a mixture of both positive and negative aspects. If they weren't, the positive ones would be easy to maneuver through and hold on to, and the negative ones would be easy to discard because it would be apparent how terrible and unhealthy they are. The truth is that relationships fall in a gray area, as you'll see in the exercise below. A "perfect" relationship would have a balance of positive and negative factors, but very few relationships are balanced, which means they tend to lean in a positive or negative direction. Relationships in the gray area may sound frustrating, confusing, and frightening to identify and live with, and they can be, especially for those with BPD. You may want your relationships to be black and white, and attempting to force them to be so is a part of your BPD holding you in place.

Tony examined his relationship with his mom and found the confounding gray area we just discussed. Though she provided him food and shelter growing up, she was also verbally and emotionally abusive. This reality forced Tony to grapple with how to characterize his relationship with her. In the end he determined it was highly negative (see figure 10).

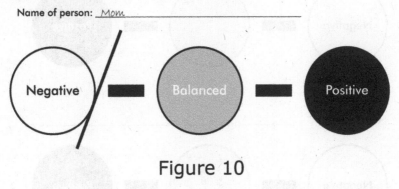

Figure 10

Using the Relationship Scale (figure 11), write the names of three people you're in a relationship with. They can be people you identified in the previous two exercises, such as a family member, a child, a romantic partner, or a coworker, or someone you didn't identify. Then, determine where on the scale you think the relationship falls and make a slash. The slash doesn't have to occur in one of the bubbles. As I mentioned, most relationships are not black and white—that is, they fall in the gray area between absolutes. You can download a blank copy of the scale at http://www.newharbinger.com/42730, so you can do this exercise for as many relationships as you like.

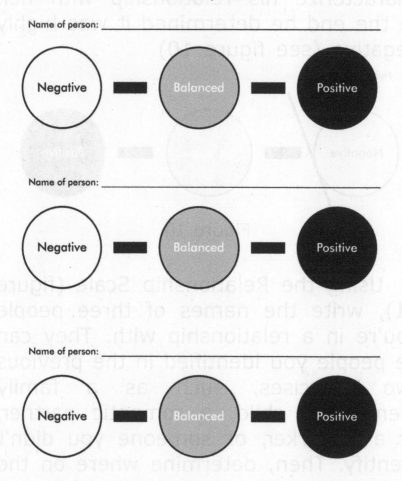

Relationship Scale

Keeping in mind how you rated the three relationships you identified, answer these self-exploration questions.

What could you do to make your relationships less negative?

_____

_____

_____

What could you do to make your relationships more positive?

_____

_____

_____

Tony tended to engage in behaviors that kept him in difficult and abusive relationships, feeling overwhelmed and lonely, and stuck in place with his BPD. He was often confused about how he felt about himself and the behaviors he engaged in, and he felt powerless to change how he treated himself and others, and he couldn't understand why. When he explored his relationships, he was able to discover that he kept negative people around him, and that these relationships kept him stuck in a cycle of self-destruction and dependency on others for love and care. Using the exercises in this chapter, Tony identified those people who were healthy, made him feel good about himself, and encouraged him to grow.

Remember, most relationships operate in the realm of shades of gray, not all good and not all bad. The key factor in all of your relationships is you, and that's a good and powerful thing. You're the one who can continue to build your relationships, and you can choose to change or end the negative ones. Changing negative relationships doesn't entail allowing, accepting, or making compromises for the negatives, rather the goal is to try to make more positive factors. If you choose to do this, keep in mind that encouraging positive factors isn't possible in all relationships, and those are the ones you have to leave behind. Your BPD is comfortable in those negative relationships, because they feed it, and your BPD is always hungry. The goal of this workbook is to help you grow beyond your BPD, and discarding negative relationships is a critical factor for doing this.

Solidifying Steps to Growth

Using the spaces below, pull together what you learned from this chapter so you can take this information with you.

The most helpful information I learned from this chapter:

1. _____
2. _____
3. _____

The skills that I want to practice:

1. _____
2. _____
3. _____

While going through this chapter, I was thinking _____, and it helped me to see that _____

_____
_____

You made it to the end of part 2 of the workbook! Strengthening your readiness and taking steps to grow beyond your BPD is an awesome achievement. To help strengthen what you've learned, there's a summary available for download at http://www.n ewharbinger.com/42730. This summary pulls together the concepts, activities, and exercises from part 2 of the workbook, so I highly recommend that you take the time to go through it before moving on to part 3.

You've completed the first two parts of this workbook. Good work! It's time to address and change those negative beliefs, behaviors, and patterns that cause you problems and hold you back. Before we move forward, I want you to take a break and reward yourself with something fun and positive. I like to reward myself with a slice of cheesecake. What will you choose?

PART 3

Addressing and Changing Negative Behaviors and Patterns of BPD

CHAPTER 10

Freedom from the Trap of Emotional Buttons

In this chapter you're going to learn how to break free from *emotional buttons*—those things that hit you to your core, that bring up all those past thoughts, feelings, and memories that make you feel like you've been pulled back in time to a past experience. We'll explore their roots and how they influence your thoughts, feelings, and memories today, and you'll learn ways to control and respond to them.

Emotional Buttons: Rooted in the Past

You may be thinking that emotional buttons sound just like triggers (see chapter 8). Triggers are similar to emotional buttons in that they distort how we see and react to the world, but emotional buttons are tied to specific situations or events from the past that shaped how you see and react to the world in the present. Buttons are from a deeper place inside you that gets activated, and when they get pressed the urge to react carries greater emotional weight than do triggers. Emotional button reactions that occur repeatedly create patterns of negative beliefs and behaviors that cause problems in all areas of your life.

Betty's emotional buttons are rooted in her childhood. Growing up she was often left home alone while her mother went out, or she was locked in her room when her mom brought men home. In addition to leaving Betty in risky (and lonely) situations, and on her own to get her needs met, Betty's mom always put others first when her daughter needed to emotionally connect. This left Betty feeling abandoned and empty inside.

Over time, these feelings developed into emotional buttons. When they were pushed, Betty acted out by harming herself or others in an attempt to get her needs met and to make the feelings of abandonment and loneliness go away. She fell into dysfunctional patterns of behavior to cope with the pain of feeling abandoned and disrespected. Eventually, her worldview became distorted, and she tended to see present-day situations and circumstances through the lens of a past full of loneliness and failed attempts to get her needs met.

For example, when some of Betty's friends didn't respond to her text quickly enough, she cut her arms. When her boyfriend failed to show up on time, she went online to find someone to hook up with. Had she instead explored these situations in the present moment, she would have realized that poor cell service prevented her texts from going through, and that her boyfriend was late because he'd been stuck in traffic and his cell phone battery had died. Instead, when he arrived and saw that she was online looking for a hookup, they argued, and he walked away very angry, leaving Betty feeling even more abandoned and empty inside.

When they're pushed, emotional buttons act like a fog rolling in over your senses, causing you to misinterpret the present and react based upon the past. You feel an intense emotional push to react, and this is due to being caught up in what was and *not* what is.

Identifying Your Emotional Button Response

To avoid being activated by your emotional buttons, you have to determine what thoughts, feelings, and memories are connected to them; the patterns of beliefs and behaviors you are pushed to engage in; and the past experiences that created them, including how these experiences impact you in the present and how you see your future. Because you react so fast when your buttons are pushed, you may not realize that a sequence of responses is actually engaged. The more you're able to break down and identify the elements of this sequence, the more you'll be able control it. The following series of exercises will help you do this.

Take your time going through these exercises. Do them over a series of days if you need to. By the end, you'll have some very useful, empowering information. You can download the complete worksheet sequence at http://www.newharbinger.com/42730, in the summary for part 3 of the workbook.

Identify your button-pushing situations. What happens in your life today that sets you off, making you feel like you did when you were younger and in a particular situation? Identify as many button-pushing situations as you can. We'll start with an example from Betty.

My emotional buttons are pushed when: *My friends don't text me back. Also, when my boyfriend is late and doesn't call me. When people don't respond to me when and how I expect them to.*

My emotional buttons are pushed when: _____
_____
_____

The situations you listed above push your emotional buttons. Now that you've identified them, let's take a look at what thoughts, feelings, and memories are connected to them.

Identify the thoughts, feelings, and memories that come up. In the spaces below, write down the thoughts, feelings, and memories that you experience when your buttons are pushed. Give as much detail as you can, and try not to edit your responses too much. You're just gathering information here. We'll start with an example from Betty.

Emotional button: *My friends don't text me back or my boyfriend doesn't show up when he's supposed to.*

My emotional button thoughts: *No one cares about me. I'm not important to anyone. I'm useless—not worth a text or call.*

My emotional button feelings: *I feel alone, abandoned, forgotten, unimportant, and empty inside.*

My emotional button memories: *I remember my mom leaving me all alone at home or locked in my room while she spent time with her boyfriends.*

Emotional button: _____
_____

My emotional button thoughts:
_____

My emotional button feelings: _____

My emotional button memories: _____

Emotional button: _____

My emotional button thoughts:

My emotional button feelings: _____

My emotional button memories: _____

Emotional button: _____

My   emotional   button   thoughts:
_____

My emotional button feelings: _____

My   emotional   button   memories:
_____

Identify the negative beliefs, behaviors, or patterns that are connected to your emotional buttons. These beliefs, behaviors, and patterns can include outward reactions toward others, such as yelling, throwing things, hitting walls and other people, and so on. They can also involve inward reactions, such as using drugs or alcohol, self-harming, saying bad things about you to yourself, and so on. We'll start with an example from Betty.

Emotional button: *My friends don't text me back or my boyfriend doesn't show up when he's supposed to.*

My   emotional   button   beliefs: *My belief is that I'm going to be alone forever, and no one will ever want to be close to me.*

My emotional button behaviors: *My behaviors are that I'll write a flaming text to my friends who I think are ignoring me, or I'll cut my arms. Or if my boyfriend's late and doesn't call, I might go out and look for hookups and not even care if I'm safe.*

My emotional button patterns: *My pattern is that every time I feel abandoned and empty I act self-destructively—cutting myself or having unsafe sex and cheating on my boyfriend.*

Emotional button: _____

_____

My emotional button beliefs: _____

_____

_____

My emotional button behaviors: _____

_____

_____

My emotional button patterns: _____

_____

_____

Emotional button: _____

My emotional button beliefs: _____

My emotional button behaviors: _____

My emotional button patterns: _____

Emotional button: _____

My emotional button beliefs: _____

My emotional button behaviors: _____

My emotional button patterns: _____

Identify the associations between your emotional buttons and your past, present, or future. Breaking down the associations between past pain and present behavior helps you understand what drives you to have negative beliefs or to engage in the negative behaviors and patterns that have kept your BPD active for so long. Understanding past pain, present behavior, and future expectations helps you to control your emotional buttons by slowing down and choosing to not engage in default, immediate, and unhealthy responses when you're triggered. But first you have to know everything your buttons are connected to.

By doing this exercise, Betty was able to work out that her fear of abandonment and feeling of emptiness were related to the neglect she'd experienced (past). This fear and feeling influenced her perception of the intentions of her friends and boyfriend (present). Her repeated experience of feeling abandoned and empty fed her beliefs that she'd be alone forever and would never be treated with respect (future). Here's how she answered this part of the exercise.

Emotional button: *My friends don't text me back or my boyfriend doesn't show up when he's supposed to.*

My emotional button's connection to the past: *I remember my mom leaving me all alone at home or locked in my room while she spent time with her boyfriends. I felt abandoned and empty when my mom chose her own needs over mine—which was almost all the time.*

My emotional button's connection to the present: *I feel abandoned and empty when my friends and boyfriend blow me off, or when I think they're blowing me off, which is not always true.*

My emotional button's connection to the future: *I feel so sure this is how it's always going to be. Because why would it change? How could it?*

Let's explore how your emotional buttons connect to your past, impact your present, and influence your expectations of the future. Be as descriptive as you can, be patient with yourself, and take breaks if you need to. Do this at your own pace and in a way that fits for you.

Emotional button: _____

My emotional button's connection to the past: _____

My emotional button's connection to the present: _____

My emotional button's connection to the future: _____

Emotional button: _____

My emotional button's connection to the past: _____

My emotional button's connection to the present: _____

My emotional button's connection to the future: _____

_____

_____

Emotional button: _____

My emotional button's connection to the past: _____

My emotional button's connection to the present: _____

My emotional button's connection to the future: _____

_____

_____

Being able to uncover the sequence from emotional button to thoughts, feelings, and memories to beliefs, behaviors, and patterns to how they're linked to your past, present, and future is a powerful skill. When you know what your emotional buttons mean, and the influence they have on you, you're empowered to manage your responses and to choose to not engage in negative patterns. This lessens the control BPD has over you. Now that you know what some of your emotional buttons are and all that they impact, you're ready to learn skills to manage how you respond to them.

Managing Your Emotional Button Responses

When first learning how to manage your emotional button responses, the secret to success is this:

Strike while the iron's cold.

In other words, when you're first learning to manage your responses, don't work on them while they're happening. Only work on them when you're not activated or overwhelmed. When the "iron" of your emotional reaction is hot, it's hard to handle. When it has cooled down, it's manageable—you can "touch" it without getting burned. There's room to maneuver, emotionally speaking. Black belts in karate approach training like this. They train for countless hours, building new skills. Then when they have a match—when things are "hot"—their mind and body are ready. It's best to approach learning how to manage emotional button responses the same way. You practice and train so when the challenge comes, you're better able to control yourself, act differently, and influence the outcome so it's more likely to be in your favor.

Before we get to the specific strategies, we have to plan when and with whom we're most likely to need these strategies—when our iron is likely to heat up. Karate masters think about possible scenarios in which they may have to use their training, and so should you. Use the space below to identify the people and situations that push your buttons.

The people most likely to push my buttons are: _____

_____

_____

The situations in which I'm most likely to have my emotional buttons pushed are: _____

_____

_____

Below are three management strategies that will help you when your emotional buttons get pushed. Pick the one (or ones) that feels like a good fit with your lifestyle and interests, and practice it every day, several times a day.

Break Time

This strategy is about taking a break when your buttons have been pushed, so you can stop what you're doing and remove yourself from the situation. Depending on the context, to get your break time you could say, "Excuse me, I need to go to the restroom," or "I need to make a call," or "I want to hear what you're saying, and I'll be back. I just have to take care of something first, and then I'll be able to give you my full attention." Once you've removed yourself from the situation, find a safe place to collect your thoughts. For example, if you're at work or at a restaurant, you can excuse yourself, go to the bathroom, and breathe.

During your break, remember that your emotional buttons are about *what was and not what is.* Stay aware of the here and now, and allow the emotional buttons to deactivate. It might help to imagine that you're a karate master, floating on a cloud in the here and now, focusing on the present, and deactivating your emotional buttons as your iron grows colder and colder and you become more and more in control. You might also look online for images that represent your break time and your iron cooling down.

Practice these techniques multiple times during the day. In the spaces below, design your break time in advance by writing out the places you can go, what you can say to remove yourself, and what images will work for you when your emotional buttons are pressed. Try to imagine the people (friends or family members) who and situations (at work or while online) that tend to push your buttons. The more preparation you do, the more likely you are to maintain your focus and control when your buttons are pressed.

Statements for taking my break time: _____
_____

_____

During my break time, I'll imagine and practice: _____
_____

_____

Self-Statements of Truth

Self-statements of truth are the positive and honest things you say to yourself when your emotional buttons are pressed, such as *I'm safe, I don't have to do anything I don't want to do, I'm in control of my choices,* or *This is just my past talking. This isn't really what I think it is.* These statements are meant to calm you, but they also empower you to manage the situation. Use the space below to list your self-statements of truth (you can use the ones above or make up your own) and when and where you plan to practice them. Remember, lots of practice in lots of different situations is the best way to build this skill.

My self-statements of truth: _____

_____

_____

_____

When and where I'll practice them:

_____

_____

_____

_____

Strategic Distraction

Strategic distraction is a great technique for when you feel your emotional buttons have been pressed. Some examples include starting a conversation with a safe and positive person (someone who's encouraging, who isn't going to focus on the negatives), reading a book, going for a walk, playing a game on your phone, going to an AA or NA meeting (if you're in either program), and so on. The purpose is to direct your attention away from your thoughts, feelings, and memories so you can, in a controlled manner, collect yourself and reengage with the person or situation that pressed your emotional button. Try to think of some strategic distraction techniques that might work for you.

My strategic distraction techniques:

_____

_____

The more you plan for and practice button-pressing situations with different people, the more skill you'll develop and the more choice and control you'll have so you can respond differently.

Responding Differently to Your Emotional Buttons

Your emotional buttons are rooted in *what was and not what is,* and they appear to cause an immediate reaction based upon past experiences. Although it's hard to recognize when you're in the middle of it, there is a bit of time between your emotional button being pushed and your response. So far in this chapter you've explored what your emotional buttons are, where they originated, and what happens when they're pushed. You've planned and practiced strategies for managing them, and now it's time to empower yourself to respond differently.

Betty's immediate response to her emotional buttons being pushed was to cut herself or to go online to find someone she could hook up with. She found that she liked doing the break time strategy. When her emotional buttons were pushed and she felt the impulse to go to the Internet or to cut herself, she instead went outside and took a walk. While she walked, she opened her phone and looked at the funny cartoon picture of a karate master she'd downloaded to remind herself to respond as a karate master would: in a calm and collected way. This helped her to see the situation clearly. As she felt her mind clear, she reminded herself, *This is about my past with my mom, not about my present with my boyfriend.* This technique allowed her to cool down. By doing this, she was able to answer the door when her boyfriend arrived and ask him why he was late and why he hadn't responded when she called. She was able to hear his response and not argue with him, and they were then able to have a great time together.

In the following exercise, let's explore what happens when your buttons are pushed and how you can respond differently. First, identify an emotional button, then describe how you usually respond when it's pushed, and, finally, think of another way to respond. Use the management strategies discussed in this chapter to help you, or use one of the other strategies we've discussed in the workbook, such as mindfulness or the "let it out" list. Be as descriptive as possible in your responses. Write down whatever you think, because there are no wrong answers.

Emotional button: _____

_____

When my emotional button is pushed, I usually ... _____

_____
_____
_____

To respond differently, I will ...
_____

Your BPD has used emotional button responses to control you, but this chapter has given you some powerful new ways to manage them, and to grow beyond your BPD. As you develop the skill of being able to clearly see situations and circumstances through the distortion of your emotional buttons, you'll have more opportunities for control and success.

Challenge and Change Plan

Using the spaces below, pull together what you learned from this chapter so you can take this information with you.

The most helpful information I learned from this chapter:

1. _____

2. _____

3. _____

The skills that I want to practice:

1. _____

2. _____

3. _____

While going through this chapter, I was thinking _____, and it helped me to see that _____

_____

_____

Controlling your emotional buttons is very empowering, and taking this skill forward with you is important because you're going to continue to encounter situations that will challenge and stress you. In the next chapter, as you continue your journey of overcoming BPD, we're going to discuss these high-stress situations.

CHAPTER 11

Controlling High-Risk Situations

As you've made your way through this workbook, you've learned to challenge your BPD beliefs, behaviors, and patterns and to grow beyond them. In this chapter, we'll continue this journey by identifying and exploring the typical high-risk situations in which you lose control and your BPD makes decisions for you, decreasing the probability of a successful outcome. You can probably think of a few of these situations right now. Perhaps they are with a family member at dinner, a significant other when you're out on a date, a coworker in the breakroom or during a meeting, or with a stranger in line at the grocery store. To manage these high-risk situations in your life, you need to understand what they are, plan for what you're going to do when they arise, and learn to respond using adaptive and healthy behaviors that decrease the probability of you falling into your negative beliefs, behaviors, and patterns. I'll cover these topics in depth in this chapter.

Identifying High-Risk Situations

Welch and Linehan (2002) identified common high-risk situations for individuals diagnosed with BPD that prompt them to engage in drug use or self-harm behaviors. These situations include interpersonal interactions, negative emotions, life events, cognitive distress, and cues and urges, all of which I detail in this section. Though these experts only identified drug use and self-harm, their findings are relevant for the many other negative behaviors that people with BPD tend to engage in when they're in high-risk situations.

As you read through this chapter, keep in mind that you may experience two or more high-risk situations at the same time. When this happens, you may feel even more overwhelmed than normal, causing you to have a greater tendency to respond with negative beliefs, behaviors, and patterns. But you can control your responses with awareness and planning, both of which are key to creating a more positive outcome for yourself regardless of how many high-risk situations you find yourself in at any one time.

Interpersonal Interactions

High-risk interpersonal interactions tend to involve a lot of conflict and are linked to specific individuals and associated thoughts, feelings, or beliefs. They typically occur when you feel you've lost the support of a friend, loved one, or family member and feel worthless, abandoned, rejected, and so on.

One of Tony's high-risk interpersonal interactions involved wanting to be closer to his girlfriends than they wanted to be to him. This interaction activated his fear of being alone, worthless, and unrecognized. For example, when he tried to get closer to Pam too quickly, she distanced herself from him. As she pulled away, he then tried harder to win her love and be closer to her—calling and texting her repeatedly when asked not to, showing up unannounced at her work and professing his undying love for her. But his efforts only pushed her further away—the opposite of what he wanted.

In the space below, identify the individuals and associated thoughts, feelings, and beliefs that tend to make up or create your high-risk interpersonal interactions, and describe what tends to happen in these interactions. Put in as much detail as you can, and use more paper if you need to.

_____

_____

_____

_____

Negative Emotions

Negative emotions include anger, anxiety, stress, guilt, loneliness, helplessness, shame, and feelings of being trapped, to name a few. With BPD, these emotions tend to overwhelm you, causing you to have a hard time seeing anything adaptive or positive about yourself, others, and situations. This may cause you to fall into your negative beliefs, behaviors, and patterns, destroying your ability to see clearly and to grow, which is what your BPD wants so *it* can continue to thrive.

Tony's negative emotions of self-hate, doubt, and contempt for his life and his abilities came up after talking to, or spending time with, his mother. When he felt this way, he fell into his negative patterns of calling himself worthless and incompetent, and he tended to neglect all other things in his life. This caused other people to feel neglected and to pull away, because he appeared inconsistent and uncaring, the opposite of how he felt and of how he wanted to be perceived.

In the space below, write about the negative emotions, such as fear, loneliness, abandonment, and anxiety, that prompt you to engage in your negative beliefs, behaviors, and patterns, and about how you tend to react when you have these emotions. Put in as much detail as you can, and use more paper if you need to.

_____

_____

_____

_____

_____

Life Events

High-risk life events include divorce, unemployment, death of a loved one, end of a relationship, personal injury, financial problems, imprisonment, or anything that causes significant physical or psychological pain and discomfort.

Tony experienced a cascade of high-risk life events. He was fired from his job and had to move back in with his mother. She then criticized him for his "laziness," making him feel worthless, even though he was continually trying to find work. In the middle of all this, his girlfriend left him. Eventually, Tony fell back into his negative pattern of abusing alcohol and intensely trying to find a new girlfriend.

In the space below, describe your high-risk life events in as much detail as you can and what you did when they occurred. Put in as much detail as you can, and use more paper if you need to.

_____

_____

_____

_____

_____

Cognitive Distress

Cognitive distress entails negative thoughts and memories you can't get out of your mind that are related to fear, danger, past trauma, or stressful events. It causes intense anxiety, uneasiness, agitation, and so on.

Tony would often say that he was "haunted" by the loss of his father. His guidance counselor in elementary school had to tell him about his father's death because his mother refused to speak about it. When Tony had memories of being in elementary school and learning of his father, they were intense, like a flashback. As a result, he often would drink alone until he passed out, but when he woke up he still remembered why he drank so much.

In the space below, in as much detail as you can or feel comfortable doing, write about your high-risk cognitive distress and what you tend to do when you feel it. If this gets too difficult or you feel overwhelmed, take a break, talk to a positive friend or a mental health provider, and come back to this exercise when you feel ready. Use more paper if you need to.

Cues and Urges

Cues and urges are those things in the environment that influence your thoughts, feelings, and memories in ways that drive you to respond using your negative beliefs, behaviors, and patterns.

When Tony went online to look at social media, he would often see his friends and ex-girlfriends having good times with others, going exciting places, and doing things he wished he was doing (his cue). As he looked at these images, he felt compelled to call and text his girlfriend to try and have the experiences and perceived happiness he was seeing online (his urge). This cue and urge started a sequence of thoughts about being alone and unloved, and these thoughts led to feelings of isolation, worthlessness, and depression. These feelings felt valid because of memories of his mother saying hurtful things, and of past girlfriends leaving him and wanting nothing to do with him. In response to these feelings Tony would repeatedly call and text his girlfriend until she responded, and if she didn't, he'd go to her job and try to talk to her, which pushed her further away, when all he wanted was to be close to her and to experience the great lives he believed he was seeing online.

In the space below, write about your high-risk cues and urges. Put in as much detail as you can, and use more paper if you need to.

Identifying Alternative Behaviors

Now that you've identified your BPD high-risk situations, you can learn how to effectively manage and control them by identifying and applying positive, adaptive alternative behaviors. Being prepared with adaptive and healthy alternatives will significantly decrease the likelihood of you falling into negative beliefs, behaviors, and patterns. Let's start by identifying viable alternative behaviors. You can download additional copies of this worksheet at http://www .newharbinger.com/42730.

Alternative Behaviors List

Write a checkmark next to the alternative behaviors that you think might work for you when you find yourself in high-risk situations. There are spaces at the end for you to write in your own.

☐ Make a list of things you can do that are healthy, such as take a walk, play with your dog or cat, play a game on your phone, or go to the bathroom to have a moment to catch your breath.

☐ Reach out to a safe and positive friend or loved one.

☐ Remove yourself from the high-risk situation.

☐ Make a list of all the benefits of *not* falling into your negative patterns.

☐ Practice a mindfulness exercise (see chapter 8).

☐ Practice the "let it out" list (see chapter 8).

☐ Make a list of what you're grateful for and then review it.

☐ Treat yourself to a reward for not engaging in your negative patterns. For example, buy yourself a latte or an ice cream cone or go to a movie (something funny and positive that encourages a positive mood).

☐ Smell an essential oil, such as lavender, cinnamon, or cedarwood, that helps you refocus and calms you down.

☐ Create and play a playlist with motivating or calming music.

☐ Smile—it actually reduces the body's stress response (Kraft and Pressman 2012).

☐ Other: _____

☐ Other: _____

☐ Other: _____

Hopefully you found some behavior options for your high-risk situations. To master these new behaviors and make them your default responses, you'll need to practice them as often as you can. Now we'll move to applying your new alternative behaviors to your high-risk situations.

Replacing Behaviors in High-Risk Situations

In this exercise you'll pair some of the high-risk situations you've identified for yourself with alternative behaviors that will help you control your reaction and make adaptive and healthy choices. If it seems like it'd be helpful, review your responses to the preceding exercises. Respond as best you can, and don't edit your responses. There are no wrong answers, nor is there anything to be embarrassed about or ashamed of. This is about your growth, so be honest with yourself—you deserve it. You can download a copy of this worksheet at http://www.newharbinger.com/42730.

If I experience the high-risk situation of _____, I can now use these adaptive and healthy alternative behaviors: _____

_____

_____

If I experience the high-risk situation of _____, I can now use these adaptive and healthy alternative behaviors: _____

_____

_____

Learning new skills takes time and patience. I understand that it can be difficult, particularly for individuals with BPD, but replacing negative beliefs, behaviors, and patterns with adaptive and healthy ones is an important part of the growth process. If you can, practice using the alternative behaviors you identified above two to three times a day. If you can't physically do this, then practice them in your mind; this is a great way to build skills too.

Challenge and Change Plan

Using the spaces below, pull together what you learned from this chapter so you can take this information with you.

The most helpful information I learned from this chapter:

1. _____

2. _____

3. _____

The skills that I want to practice:

1. _____

2. _____

3. _____

While going through this chapter, I was thinking _____, and it helped me to see that _____
_____

_____

Now that you've learned about managing high-risk situations and developed a plan for engaging in adaptive and healthy alternative behaviors, you'll have greater control over your BPD when those high-risk situations occur and be better equipped to make choices that increase the likelihood of positive outcomes. This helps to set the stage for challenging and changing the dysfunctional beliefs that support your BPD.

CHAPTER 12

Challenging and Changing Dysfunctional Beliefs

Many of your negative patterns are rooted in dysfunctional beliefs that developed alongside your BPD. It's time to start changing those beliefs.

Much of the content of this chapter is derived from self-determination theory, which proposes that people are driven to better themselves and correct areas of difficulty in life—to which dysfunctional beliefs certainly contribute (Ryan and Deci 2002). In this chapter, you're going to learn to recognize your dysfunctional beliefs, challenge their accuracy, identify evidence that shows they're untrue, and counter them with healthy and adaptive beliefs. This process will help you weaken them and grow beyond them, allowing you to continue on this path of growth beyond your BPD.

Your Dysfunctional Beliefs

Dysfunctional beliefs distort our perceptions and impact how we see the world. Our distorted perceptions drive our reactions, which in turn affect our relationships, self-control, and beliefs about ourselves. These beliefs tend to become automatic, and very powerful. Extensive research has shown that challenging and changing beliefs increases one's ability to do things differently and to change life for the better (Ciarrochi 2004; Clark 2014; Delavechia et al. 2016).

But it's not easy. Identifying dysfunctional beliefs can be like discovering that friends you once counted on are actually harmful for you and don't have your best interest at heart. To start, you have to acknowledge that these beliefs are a part of your BPD, which has caused you confusion and conflict in many areas of your life. But at this point in the workbook, you're ready and able to pull back the curtain in order to identify them.

Let's take a look at a couple of Betty's dysfunctional beliefs: "I must be liked at all times" and "I must be perfect at all times or no one will like me."

When Betty started a new nursing job, it seemed to her that all of her new coworkers were very close to each other but not accepting of her. She drew these conclusions because, as her first day on the job progressed, people greeted her but wouldn't really stop to talk and get to know her. She watched everyone else laugh and joke with each other, and she started to believe that they were laughing and joking about her and sharing their judgments about how "stupid" she must be. As these thoughts gained force, she couldn't focus on her job.

She made a minor mistake on a patient's chart, as parts of the computer system used in the office were new to her, and other employees had to help her fix it. This mistake, coupled with her inexperience, only justified the accuracy of her dysfunctional beliefs, causing increased anxiety, frustration, and anger. One of the nurses who had helped her told her, "If you need anything, just let me know." Betty misinterpreted this, and heard, "I know you're too stupid to do this job, so when you need more help, which you will, I will fix your mistake again." Feeling she had to defend herself against the attack, Betty jumped up and pushed the other nurse. Her new boss saw this and fired Betty on the spot.

Have you ever been in a situation similar to Betty's, in that your dysfunctional beliefs had a significant negative impact on how you interpreted your environment? If so, you're not alone! Change is possible, and it comes about when you build your sense of self-determination, learning what is true about yourself and what you want to achieve, and then using that knowledge to challenge dysfunctional beliefs to have better control of yourself and how you see the world. Here's the process:

Identify your dysfunctional beliefs.

↓

Challenge those beliefs.

↓

Change your dysfunctional beliefs.

Let's go through the process with your own beliefs.

Identifying Your Dysfunctional Beliefs

Let's take a closer look at the value of identifying dysfunctional beliefs using Betty's situation at her new job.

Betty allowed her dysfunctional beliefs ("I must be liked at all times" and "I must be perfect at all times or no one will like me") to distort her experience at her new job. The dysfunctional beliefs took over, and she got caught up thinking that people were talking about and judging her. Anxiety quickly overwhelmed her, and she couldn't clearly see what was happening or accurately hear what the other nurse had said to her. Her intense anxiety pushed her to react inappropriately, in service of her dysfunctional beliefs.

Had she identified her dysfunctional beliefs before her first day on the job, she would have known when they were triggering her and seen that they were causing her to stray from her goal: keeping her new job. If she'd been able to challenge her dysfunctional beliefs and replace them with functional beliefs ("I'm a great nurse," "I can do this job well," "Everyone makes mistakes and no one is perfect, so it's possible to be liked even if I'm not perfect all the time"), she might have navigated her first day successfully. Instead, her dysfunctional beliefs pushed her to be painfully, disastrously reactive, and she was fired.

As this story shows, dysfunctional beliefs can have severe consequences, so it's of utmost importance to identify yours. Below is a list of common dysfunctional beliefs. Circle the ones that fit for you, being as honest and open as you can. There are spaces to add your own unique beliefs to the list.

- People, including me, can't change.
- People are always unkind.

- I'm lazy.
- I must be perfect at all times.
- I'll never be happy.
- If anything can go wrong, it will.
- I'm stupid if I make a mistake.
- I should have done better.
- Life, the world, and other people should be fair.
- I must get everything done today.
- Others should be more polite.
- I should be living in a better place by now.
- You disrespect me by not doing what I want.
- If you valued me, I would be earning more money.
- I must not make a mistake.
- I must cope with everything.
- I must be in control of all situations.
- Things must go well.
- Others must always treat me well.
- I'm just no good.
- _____
  _____
- _____
  _____

Identifying your dysfunctional beliefs can bring up many thoughts, feelings, and memories, which are important to recognize. Many of your dysfunctional beliefs have origins in your past, and identifying the connected thoughts, feelings, and memories can help clear the confusion and conflict these distorted beliefs bring to your world. Using the prompts below, identify the thoughts, feelings, and memories the exercise above brought up for you.

Identifying my dysfunctional beliefs brought up these thoughts:

_____
_____
_____

Identifying my dysfunctional beliefs brought up these feelings:

_____
_____
_____

Identifying my dysfunctional beliefs brought up these memories:

_____
_____
_____

Challenging Your Dysfunctional Beliefs

Dysfunctional beliefs live by untruths and thrive in the dark—the unchallenged and unexplored parts of your BPD. They cause you to believe you're broken, useless, worthless, empty, and inept, among other things. But they're weakened by evidence that shows they're inaccurate. To challenge and change them, you have to shine a light on them. Identifying them was the first step; let's now uncover the concrete evidence that shows they're untrue.

Use this exercise to identify the clear evidence in your life that proves your dysfunctional beliefs are *untrue.* Clear evidence is based on identifiable facts—something that can be proven—rather than guesses or theories. I provided Betty's examples to help you get started. You can download a copy of this exercise at http://www.newharb inger.com/42730, so you can explore each dysfunctional belief you've identified for yourself.

My dysfunctional belief is that *I must be liked at all times,* but it's untrue because *even when my friends and boyfriend get mad at me, we end up making up, and they don't leave me forever.*

My dysfunctional belief is that *I must be perfect at all times or no one will like me,* but it's untrue because *I've had many fights with Sara, and we're still friends after all these years. When I dented the fender of James's car, he didn't like it, but he told me he still loved me, and I believed him.*

My dysfunctional belief is that _____, but it's untrue because _____

_____

My dysfunctional belief is that _____, but it's untrue because _____

_____

Changing Your Dysfunctional Beliefs

Changing beliefs is a process and not a "one and done" activity. It took many years and continual exposure for your dysfunctional beliefs to gain so much power over you and your life. The process to change them involves identifying and empowering your adaptive and healthy beliefs. The first step is identification, so circle the adaptive and healthy beliefs on the list below that speak to you. If you think of one that isn't listed, just add it to the list.

- I have the power to achieve my goals.
- I deserve to be treated kindly and with care.
- I am good and I have value.
- I work hard to get what I want.
- I am worth respect and love.
- I forgive myself.
- Mistakes are human and acceptable.
- I will be patient with myself.
- I am doing the best I can.
- I define me.

- I respect myself and my choices.
- I'm learning and growing every day.
- My kindness is my strength.
- I choose to support and care for myself.
- I deserve to feel good and happy.
- I can choose my own thoughts and beliefs.
- I accept my flaws, because they help me grow.
- I will exercise self-compassion.
- I deserve to be around those who build me up.
- I trust my abilities.
- I'm more than this BPD!
- _____
- _____

Now that you've identified adaptive and healthy beliefs, it's time to pair them with your weakened, old dysfunctional beliefs. By doing this, you're zeroing in on replacement beliefs that will encourage, empower, and vitalize the accurate and honest part of you—the part that's not connected to your BPD.

Here's an example of Betty's:

My old dysfunctional beliefs are *I must be liked at all times and I must be perfect at all times or no one will like me.*

My adaptive and healthy beliefs to counter these are *I am good and I have value, regardless of who likes me. Mistakes don't define me; I define me, and that's enough for people to like me.*

When Betty challenged and replaced her dysfunctional beliefs, they lost their power. By doing this routinely, and learning other techniques, she was better able to control them and her associated BPD behaviors. As she built up her skills, she was able to maintain employment; to enjoy interacting with her friends, family, and boyfriend; and to achieve more in life. In other words, she was able to reach her goals and grow beyond her BPD, as you're learning to do.

It's your turn to replace your old dysfunctional beliefs with adaptive and healthy beliefs. In the spaces below, list your old dysfunctional beliefs first. You can use the ones you identified above, or new ones you want to weaken and replace. You can download a copy of this exercise at http://www.newharbing er.com/42730.

My old dysfunctional beliefs are: _____

_____

_____

My adaptive and healthy beliefs to counter these are: _____.

_____

My old dysfunctional beliefs are: _____

_____

My adaptive and healthy beliefs to counter these are: _____

_____

Now it's time to strengthen your adaptive and healthy beliefs using the same method your dysfunctional beliefs have used all these years—repetition, repetition, repetition. I want you to repeat your adaptive and healthy beliefs to yourself as often as you can. Say them in the morning when you get up, say them on your way to lunch, say them when you lie down to go to sleep, and say them everywhere in between. Write them on sticky notes and post them around your room. Sing them in the shower. The more you say them and the more you read them, the more you will live them. As you live your adaptive and healthy beliefs, you'll find that you have greater self-control and self-understanding and less of what has empowered your BPD for so long.

Challenge and Change Plan

Using the spaces below, pull together what you learned from this chapter so you can take this information with you.

The most helpful information I learned from this chapter:

1. _____

2. _____

3. _____

The skills that I want to practice:

1. _____

2. _____

3. _____

While going through this chapter, I was thinking _____, and it helped me to see that _____

_____

_____

Now that you've developed the skills to challenge your dysfunctional beliefs and change them into adaptive and healthy ones, it's time to learn valuable self-soothing techniques that will further enhance your self-control.

CHAPTER 13

Self-Soothing to Enhance Personal Control

Can you think of times when an event or an individual triggered you, and you reacted in a way that caused you to lose a relationship, hurt yourself, fall into a depression, become overwhelmed with anxiety, and then fall back to default negative beliefs, behaviors, and patterns? What if I told you that in these situations there's a way for you to calm down, reassess the situation, and engage in a manner that increases the probability of a positive outcome? Would you be interested in learning how? Most people would answer yes, and that's what this chapter is about: teaching you self-soothing techniques to enhance your personal control in challenging situations.

Personal control is the ability people have to influence their beliefs, behaviors, and patterns in order to achieve particular outcomes. For example, when Tony felt worthless and invisible, he seemed to have little personal control over his drive to connect with romantic partners; he would text them at all hours and show up at their workplace unannounced as if he didn't have a choice. Once he learned to slow himself down using self-soothing techniques, he increased his personal control in difficult situations and was able to approach them differently.

Self-soothing is the ability to comfort yourself when you're upset or distressed, and self-soothing techniques can help calm you down, allowing you to refocus when you're triggered or your buttons are pressed. These techniques are easy to learn and don't take much time at all, which makes them very useful and beneficial. I used the analogy of striking when the iron is cold when talking about controlling your emotional buttons, and this is good advice for all the skills and techniques in this workbook, including self-soothing techniques. Striking when the iron is cold entails practicing skills and techniques multiple times a day when you're calm, not when you're in distress. Practicing before you're triggered is critical, so you're ready when someone or something is getting under your skin.

Self-Soothing Techniques

You should use the first two self-soothing techniques, mindfulness and yoga, to reduce the likelihood of your iron heating up in the first place, and the venting journal and distraction techniques are for those instances when you feel your iron heating up—when you're about to, or have been, triggered. Practice these techniques as often as you can to build a sense of mastery, so you're prepared and ready to reach the best possible outcome with a clear head, enhanced personal control, and adaptive and healthy beliefs, behaviors, and patterns.

Mindfulness

Mindfulness is the art of focusing your attention on the present and calmly recognizing and accepting your feelings, thoughts, and bodily sensations as they are in that moment. By doing this, you decrease the likelihood that you'll respond to triggers using your default negative beliefs, behaviors, and patterns that have sustained your BPD for so long. Try this seven-step mindfulness technique for one minute, or for as long as you can and need to, until you feel calm, focused, and relaxed. Like any other skill, the more you do this one the better you'll get at it.

1. Find a quiet place free of distraction.
2. Sit comfortably, with your back straight but relaxed. Close your eyes, if doing so feels comfortable.
3. Focus your attention on your breath going in and out—in through your nose, and out through your mouth.
4. Don't judge what comes to mind. Let it float in and float out.
5. Let distractions come and go, and stay as focused as you can on

your breath and being in the present moment, nothing else.

6. When you feel relaxed, notice your breath and how you feel. Open your eyes and be mindful of the present.

7. Reengage and make the decision that is best for you.

Were you able to be mindful for a full minute, paying attention to your breathing, not being distracted by thoughts, and letting distractions go? It's fine if you weren't able to. Many of us have a hard time slowing down because our world is so fast paced and we all have so many things going on at the same time. Take a moment to reflect on this exercise. Describe what it was like for you (scary, uncomfortable, relaxing, empowering) and what made it that way ("I wasn't sure what was going to happen," "I felt my anxiety lower and I could control my thoughts").

_____

_____

_____

_____

_____

Yoga

Yoga has been around for a very, very long time, and kings and kids and everyone in between have used it. Yoga can be beneficial no matter your age or mental state. It provides mental calmness, stress reduction, and body awareness, which leads to increased self-confidence and personal control. The skills you learn in yoga—controlling thoughts and focusing on breathing—can improve your mental health before, during, and after you've been triggered.

You don't have to go to a yoga class or buy the outfits, and all that other stuff, if you don't want to. You can learn about and practice yoga using free YouTube videos. These offer privacy, which might be important to you. Regardless of how you decide to give yoga a try, be it through videos or classes, try practicing yoga as often as you can to reap the most benefits.

Venting Journal

When you're triggered, do you feel the pressure build until you just can't hold it any longer and you explode in anger, either verbally or physically? The venting journal is a technique for releasing all of your negative thoughts and feelings without editing or holding back. It offers unrestrained opportunities to get it out, express yourself, examine what upset you, and develop a sense of calm and relaxation in a safe and secure way.

Your venting journal can be written or recorded, and you can keep it in a notebook, on your computer, or on your phone—anywhere you like. One great benefit of the venting journal is that you can do it any time, day or night, go on for as long as you want or need, and review it to understand yourself in the moment. It's a great tool for monitoring how you respond to particular situations.

The following prompts might help you get started, but you don't have to use these. You can write your own or freestyle without prompts, if you prefer. Do whatever works for you.

- I was triggered when...
- In the situation I felt (thought, wanted)...

- Right now, I feel...
- Before, during, and after, I thought...
- In the end, I want...
- It would be different if...
- I would feel better if...
- This situation brought up ... from the past
- The best result would be...
- This situation taught me...

Try using this technique whenever you feel your iron heating up, even if you're only triggered a little bit. When you've used the venting journal steadily for a week or so, decide if it's something you'd like to keep using going forward.

Distraction

Distraction is a very effective self-soothing technique that physically or mentally, or both, removes you from a triggering situation. Pick two or three distraction techniques from the following list that you think might really absorb you, that might pull your attention away from a triggering event or individual:

- Watch funny, uplifting, or encouraging movies or videos.
- Listen to music.
- Draw whatever comes to mind.
- Go for a long run or walk.
- Make lists of everything you have to do, things you've done, things you may want to buy, how you're going to achieve your dreams, healthy adventures you'd like to have, and so forth.
- Go dancing or play your favorite song and dance in your living room.
- Play a video game.
- Do a jigsaw or crossword puzzle.
- Clean your house.
- Take your pet for a walk or give it a bath.
- Eat one of your favorite foods.
- Count things around you, such as floor tiles, cracks in the street, chocolate chips on the top of a cookie (my favorite), and so on.
- Work in your garden.
- Smell an essential oil. (Find an essential oil you like, that you find soothing, and save it for distraction purposes. Some popular examples include lavender, cedarwood, lemon,

mandarin, and jasmine. These oils can be found online or in many grocery stores.)

- Other: _____
- Other: _____

These techniques are great for when you're triggered, but you should practice them when you're not triggered as well, to build your skill for using them when you need to be distracted, calm, and in control the most. Here are the four steps for using the techniques:

1. Recognize you were triggered.
2. Engage in the distraction technique you've chosen.
3. Reassess your thoughts and feelings to see if the drive to react negatively has lessened.

   a. If the drive has lessened, and you've identified an adaptive and healthy response to engage in, go to step 4.

   b. If it hasn't, go back to step 2.
4. Reengage in the situation, or with the individual, in a clearer state of mind: relaxed, calm, and focused using your adaptive and healthy response patterns.

Rating Self-Soothing Techniques

Now that you've learned about self-soothing techniques that can enhance your personal control, consider the likelihood of adding one or more of them to your adaptive and healthy response patterns. Which ones really clicked with you, or do you think will click with you? Circle how likely you are to use each self-soothing technique, with 0 being not at all and 5 very likely. The techniques you rate as 3 or above are the ones you should practice regularly.

Self-Soothing Techniques	Rating					
Mindfulness	0	1	2	3	4	5
Yoga	0	1	2	3	4	5
Venting journal	0	1	2	3	4	5
Distraction	0	1	2	3	4	5

Applying Self-Soothing Techniques

It's important to be able to see yourself using adaptive and healthy response patterns in difficult situations and with people who trigger you. The following log can help you see the benefit of using self-soothing techniques by identifying the outcomes related to their use. When you're able to pinpoint a positive and reinforcing outcome you're more likely to continue to use the technique that got you there, and that's what we want. You can also use this log in a hypothetical way for practice; instead of tracking an event that's just happened, imagine a trigger, the technique you might use to address it, and the outcome you expect. This type of exercise can help you prepare for real-world situations. You can download a copy of this log in the summary for part 3 at http://www.new harbinger.com/42730. I recommend keeping a copy with you at all times, because this process of tracking will help you master personal control in real-world situations.

Self-Soothing Outcome Log

In the first column, identify the triggering event or person. Next, identify the self-soothing technique you used to gain control over yourself physically or mentally, or both, instead of resorting to negative beliefs, behaviors, and patterns. Lastly, in as much detail as you can, write out the outcome you experienced having used the technique. The first one has been done for you using one of Tony's triggering events. Don't forget, you can also practice using this log with hypothetical and anticipated situations.

Triggering Event or Person	Self-Soothing Technique	Outcome
My mom triggered me by calling me a loser and saying I am worthless and lazy.	I used my venting journal on my phone.	I was able to disengage with my mom and stay calm and not get sucked into an argument.

As you complete the log, you're likely to notice that your skills for personal control and identifying better outcomes improve as you practice using self-soothing techniques. Remember, the more you practice, the greater control you'll have over your BPD and your negative beliefs, behaviors, and patterns.

Challenge and Change Plan

Using the spaces below, pull together what you learned from this chapter so you can take this information with you.

The most helpful information I learned from this chapter:

1. _____

2. _____

3. _____

The skills that I want to practice:

1. _____

2. _____

3. _____

While going through this chapter, I was thinking _____, and it helped me to see that _____

_____

Now that you've started to use skills to self-soothe and increase your personal control, you're ready to continue this journey and explore ways to strengthen love and resolve relationship conflict.

CHAPTER 14

Strengthening Love and Resolving Relationship Conflict

Many individuals with BPD struggle with relationship conflicts, issues, and satisfaction, which are connected to what we'll call relationship habits. To understand what these are, we have to first define habits and recognize their influence. *Habits* are learned behaviors that people automatically engage in when they encounter an activating event (for example, biting your nails when you're nervous about having an unexpected meeting with your boss). Habits can be bad or good, and it's possible to resolve and reduce bad habits and develop the good ones to give yourself a sense of empowerment, courage, and confidence.

Relationship habits are automatic reactions we have to people we're in relationships with, not only romantic relationships but those with friends, coworkers, and acquaintances. These responses involve our beliefs, behaviors, and patterns. Do you experience and engage in a particular belief, behavior, or pattern when you go home for the holidays and you're around your family, when you see your boss at work, or when you see a certain look on your significant other's face? These responses probably occur without you even noticing or thinking about them, because they are *developed* relationship habits. These responses can be destructive forces that cause chaos and conflict, or they can be empowering and strengthen the love, tenderness, confidence, and care you feel for yourself and others.

Your BPD has been using your relationship habits to flourish, but in this chapter you're going to learn how to strengthen the good relationship habits and reduce and resolve the destructive ones. I'm going to define the ten destructive relationship habits that reduce your relationship satisfaction and success, as well as the ten empowering relationship habits that strengthen the love and resolve you experience (or want to experience) in your relationships.

Ten Destructive Relationship Habits

Destructive relationship habits contribute to chaos and conflict and increase the negative intensity that may exist in your relationships. In the following chart, place a checkmark next to the habits that impact your relationships with your significant other, your children, your parents, your friends, your coworkers, and other people in your life. Avoid overthinking each habit or trying to determine how much each one may be present in your relationships. If you think a particular habit exists, just mark it.

✓	Habit	Impact
☐	Yelling	When we yell and scream, others close down and block out what we're trying to say, instead preparing for a counterattack. It's a misconception that the louder we are, the more others hear us.
☐	Statements of hate	When we make statements of hate, others tend to stop hearing anything else. These statements cause deep wounds that build resentment.
☐	Refusing to admit you made a mistake	When you believe firmly that you didn't or couldn't make a mistake, others tend to see you as having less integrity, which lowers trust and openness.
☐	Speaking in generalities	When we speak in unclear and general terms, others misunderstand or misinterpret what we mean. This causes others to make assumptions about what we're saying, which lessens the probability of us getting what we want and need. Speaking in generalities also encourages mind reading, which forces others to guess what we want or need.
☐	Refusing to apologize	When we refuse to apologize, even when we know we're wrong, others feel rage, anger, and resentment, which tend to cause them to see us as uncaring and untrustworthy.
☐	Finger-pointing	When we blame others for our relationship problems, they tend to become defensive, and over time this habit builds resentment.
☐	Cussing	When we use very strong and negative language, others tend to get defensive, and they don't hear what we're trying to say or understand the emotions we're trying to communicate.

✓	Habit	Impact
☐	Name-calling	When we call people hurtful names, they become angry and defensive, and over time this builds resentment. This includes "playful" name-calling, such as calling a friend a "loser" as a joke.
☐	Seeing only one side of the story	When we refuse to see the other person's viewpoint, we get lost in our own perspective of the situation and the relationship and are limited to only seeing half of what's going on.
☐	Expecting someone else to fill our "love tank"	Expecting others to fill our "love tank" puts a lot of pressure on them and the relationship. It also makes us dependent on others, and we might tend to be very anxious and cautious for fear of losing people whom we depend on.

If you marked most or all of the destructive relationship habits, don't be angry with yourself or attack yourself,

because these habits are common. Please take a moment and explore your responses.

Describe how the destructive habits you marked impact how you feel about yourself.

_____

_____

_____

_____

Describe how the destructive habits you marked impact relationships with your significant other, your children, your parents, your friends, your coworkers, and other people in your life.

_____

_____

_____

_____

How do you tend to feel after you or someone else uses a destructive relationship habit?

_____

_____

_____

_____

How do you think your significant other, your children, your parents, your friends, your coworkers, and other people in your life feel after you use a destructive relationship habit?

_____

_____

_____

Let's take a look at how destructive habits contributed to the chaos, conflict, and negative intensity in Betty's relationship. In parentheses I inserted specific habits she and Michael engaged in.

When Betty arrived home late one evening, having worked a fourteen-hour shift at the hospital, her boyfriend, Michael, calmly and clearly asked, "What happened at work? How come you're late?"

Betty was tired and felt attacked. She thought Michael was accusing her of being dishonest and unfaithful (a triggering event) and said, "I'm tired, and I don't have to justify myself to you! You're not my daddy! Who do you think you are?" (Refusing to apologize)

Michael raised his voice and sarcastically said, "Here we go again, causing problems when there aren't any! Just shut it down already!"

Betty yelled back. "You shit-heel! I hate you! You don't know a thing about what I go through each day and you just don't care." (Cussing, name-calling, yelling, seeing only one side of the story, statements of hate, speaking in generalities, and finger-pointing)

Michael's guard went up, and he yelled, "Why are you jumping all over me! I didn't even do anything wrong!" (Cussing, yelling, refusing to apologize, refusing to admit you made a mistake)

Betty continued to get upset and threw books at him, followed by the TV remote. She started to think that Michael was going to rush out of the house and leave her forever, and a feeling of emptiness began to build inside of her (expecting someone else to fill our "love tank"). The argument continued until Betty ran into the bathroom and cut herself while Michael beat on the door for her to come out.

When destructive relationship habits are used, it's not uncommon for negative reactions to intensify until there's an explosion, like the one between Betty and Michael. But relationship interactions don't have to go this way. Because personal relationships are a significant part of everyone's life, we want to develop relationship habits that empower them and resolve and reduce those habits that destroy them. Identifying your relationship habits is an important part of doing this, and of continuing to grow beyond your BPD.

It's important to mention that both Betty and Michael used destructive relationship habits. Betty was not 100 percent responsible for the relationship problems even though she was the only one working to grow beyond her BPD. You can change your relationship habits to empowering ones, but others may continue to use destructive ones. Using empowering relationship habits will increase the likelihood of a better outcome for you, and for your relationships, but you can't make someone else use them. As you make your way through this chapter and the rest of the book, remember that you can model change and growth, but it's up to other people to make their own changes.

Ten Empowering Relationship Habits

Identifying the destructive relationship habits you engage in is a powerful exercise, but it's only part of the process of changing your habits. We'll now turn to empowering relationship habits, those that inspire courage and confidence and the love, tenderness, and care you feel for yourself and others.

In the following chart, place a checkmark next to the habits that impact your relationships with your significant other, your children, your parents, your friends, your coworkers, and other people in your life. Avoid overthinking each habit or trying to determine how much each one may be present in your relationships. If you think a particular habit exists, just mark it. You want to be sure to identify any and all of the empowering habits you tend to use, so you can continue to develop them.

✓	Habit	Impact
☐	Using a calm and collected tone	When we talk to others with a tone that is low volume, slow, and steady, others are more likely to hear what we're saying, understand what we mean, and take us more seriously.
☐	Statements of compassion	When we talk to others with kindness and tenderness, they're more open, relaxed, and likely to do what we ask and provide us with what we want and need.
☐	Admitting when you make a mistake	This is a healthy and honest thing to do. Others will trust you more and feel open when talking with you.
☐	Speaking in specifics	When we're clear and specific, we're more likely to have our wants and needs met because others are more likely to understand what we want and need. Specifics remove the need for mind reading.
☐	Apologizing	When you apologize, others tend to feel that they can trust you and that you're open and honest, which increases the likelihood that they will be the same.
☐	Separating the person from the problem	Focusing on the problem and not people and their character reduces the likelihood that they'll feel compelled to defend their pride and self-esteem.
☐	Using a de-escalation approach	1. Take a breath and pause. 2. Respond wisely rather than emotionally. 3. Remind yourself that you don't have anything to prove. 4. Try to see the other person's perspective, and be open to alternative solutions other than you "winning." 5. If you must disagree, do it respectfully and be open to compromise.
☐	Examining unmet needs that are making you angry	Many arguments are not about the problem but unmet needs or hidden hurts. Communicate your needs clearly using I-messages. (For example, "I feel unimportant when you don't call to tell me you're going to be late.")
☐	Believing in a solution	Argue with a focus on a solution, not on the argument itself and winning. Know your goal for having the argument and how you, and the other person, are going to achieve a positive resolution. Getting there hand in hand is easier than having a tug-of-war to win.
☐	Loving yourself outside of the relationship	Do things that build self-confidence and an appreciation for yourself. Learn to value your self-worth without external validation. The best relationships are with two whole people, not two halves who need to connect to feel whole.

As you went through the empowering relationships habits, were you able to identify some of yours? If you found a few, that's great, but if you didn't, that's okay, because you're here to learn these skills, and you care enough about yourself and your relationships to do things differently. Please explore the impact that empowering habits have on your relationships now, or will have on your relationships as you practice using them.

Describe how the empowering habits you marked impact how you feel about yourself.

_____
_____
_____
_____

Describe how the empowering habits you marked impact relationships with your significant other, your children, your parents, your friends, your coworkers, and other people in your life.

_____
_____
_____
_____

How do you tend to feel after you or someone else uses an empowering relationship habit?

_____
_____
_____

How do you think your significant other, your children, your parents, your friends, your coworkers, and other people in your life feel after you use an empowering relationship habit?

_____

_____

Let's look at the argument Betty and Michael had, but this time through the lens of empowering relationship habits.

Betty came home from working a fourteen-hour shift at the hospital. She recognized that she was tired because she had stayed an extra two hours due to a patient emergency. As she pulled into her driveway, she took a deep breath and remembered that she had not called Michael and that he was probably worried about her (separating the person from the problem, using a de-escalation approach). She walked into the house and Michael calmly and clearly said, "What happened at work? How come you're late?"

Betty took a deep breath, recognized his statement of concern and compassion, remembered that she didn't have to prove anything, and responded, "I'm sorry. I totally forgot to call you. A patient had a seizure and someone else from the treatment team called in sick, so I stayed until we could get it under control" (using a calm and collected tone, statements of compassion, admitting when you make a mistake, speaking in specifics, and apologizing).

Michael paused for a moment, looking at her from the couch. "I know you work a lot and you give a lot to your job, but I worry that you're hurt when you don't call me. Please try to call next time, and I'm glad you're okay" (examining unmet needs that are making you angry).

Betty replied, "Thanks for understanding. I appreciate you very much. I'll be sure to call next time" (believing in a solution). As Betty walked to her room to change her clothes, she thought about how proud of herself she was that she had maintained control, addressed the issue, and avoided an argument (loving yourself outside of the relationship).

This interaction has a very different feel to it, don't you think? It doesn't feel contentious, hostile, and attacking, but calm, patient, and caring. This is what using the empowering relationship habits can do, and why they're so beneficial, encouraging you to grow beyond your BPD.

When you compare the destructive and empowering relationship habits, can you see how differently they might affect how you feel about yourself and your relationships? The destructive habits have a fierce and negative impact, while the empowering habits have a calming and "clearing of confusion" type of impact. We're now going to turn our attention to implementing these empowering relationship habits in your adaptive and healthy response patterns through imagery and practice.

Implementing Empowering Relationship Habits

Imagery is something we all use every day. How many times have you imagined how a situation will go before you get there, or how a conversation will unfold before you have it? I would bet quite a bit. You can also use imagery to unlearn old, negative, and destructive habits and to replace them with new, positive, and empowering ones. To learn any new habit, you first have to imagine yourself engaging in it. This includes learning to play a sport, play an instrument, speak a language, and so on. Breaking and replacing destructive relationship habits with empowering ones is no different than roller skating; the more you do it, the better you get at it.

Using imagery to practice empowering relationship habits can help you master them so you're ready to use them in difficult situations. Imagine using these habits in a restaurant with friends or with your significant other when problems arise, with your child's teacher when you disagree, with your friends when they're late or when you are, or with a coworker who says something you don't agree with. There are countless situations you can use for practice. To help you get started, I provided a sample scenario below, but you're welcome to use one of your own instead.

Sample scenario: I'm driving my daughter home from school, and she's in the backseat. She's screaming at me because I was late and I said I wouldn't take her to a fast-food restaurant for dinner.

1. Find a quiet place to sit and relax. Take a few deep breaths and clear your mind.
2. Imagine the other person or people (your significant other, children, parents, friends, or coworkers).
3. Imagine the environment you're in. Are you at home, at the office, in the car, on the street, or somewhere else altogether?
4. You and this other person are engaging in a discussion of your choosing. Perhaps you came home

late, like Betty. Perhaps you forgot to call the other person. Perhaps your child is acting out.

5. Visualize the empowering relationship habits you marked previously, as well as the ones you want to learn and use going forward: using a calm and collected tone, making statements of compassion, admitting when you make a mistake, speaking in specifics, apologizing, separating the person from the problem, using a de-escalation approach, examining unmet needs that are making you angry, believing in a solution, loving yourself outside of the relationship.

6. Imagine with as much detail as you can that you're responding to this other person using the empowering habits you chose.

7. You can see their response. Perhaps this person is respectful and listens to you, or perhaps he or she refuses to stop using destructive habits, but you stay the course. You stay true to your empowering habits.

8.   Take a moment and scan your body to see how you feel. Take a few deep breaths and allow yourself to relax, then reengage in your imagery.

9.   How does the situation end? Do you use the empowering habits all the way through? Does the interaction de-escalate? Do you resolve the situation calmly? Does the other person walk away?

10.   Evaluate and scan your body for how you feel after having used and stayed true to the empowering relationship habits. Do you feel less tension, anger, and rage and more hope, control, and empowerment?

Now it's your turn to identify some imagery details and scenarios you can use to practice implementing empowering relationship habits. You can download a copy of this worksheet at http://www.newharbinger.com/42730.

Imagery for Empowering Relationship Habits

1. Describe your quiet place to sit and relax.

_____

_____

_____

2. Identify the person (or people) in your scenario or situation.

_____

_____

3. Describe the environment you're in. Are you at home, at the office, in the car, on the street, or somewhere else altogether?

_____

_____

_____

4. Describe the discussion or argument you and this other person (or these other people) are engaged in.

_____

_____

5. Circle the empowering relationship habits you want to use going forward:

Using a calm and collected tone

Statements of compassion

Admitting when you make a mistake

Speaking in specifics

Apologizing

Separating the person from the problem

Using a de-escalation approach

Examining unmet needs that are making you angry

Believing in a solution

Loving yourself outside of the relationship

6. Describe in as much detail as you can how you're going to respond using the empowering habits you chose.

_____

_____

7. Describe the other person's (or people's) response in as much detail as you can.

_____

_____

8. Describe how your body feels having gone through this exercise.

9.   Describe how the situation ends in as much detail as you can.

10.   Describe how you feel having used and stayed true to the empowering relationship habits.

You can do this writing activity as often as you like. Practice the empowering relationship habits and go through the ten imagery steps as often as possible. You can use imagery while you're in your car, in the shower, on hold on the phone—really, any time you want. Try to practice at least two to three times a day, and as you master the habits you chose to work on you can choose new ones to practice with. Betty was able to do imagery exercises several times a day while she was bringing materials to nurses and doctors in the hospital, when she was in the shower, and while working out at the gym. By doing the imagery exercises, she found it was easier to implement and use the empowering relationship habits when she needed them most, and this practice helped her to continue growing beyond her BPD.

Challenge and Change Plan

Using the spaces below, pull together what you learned from this chapter so you can take this information with you.

The most helpful information I learned from this chapter:

1. _____
2. _____
3. _____

The skills that I want to practice:

1. _____
2. _____
3. _____

While going through this chapter, I was thinking _____, and it helped me to see that _____

_____

_____

You made it to the end of part 3 of the workbook! This is a wonderful accomplishment, and my hat's off to you. In this part of the workbook you gained extensive information about negative behaviors and patterns related to your BPD and learned methods to reduce their occurrence and replace them with adaptive and healthy alternatives. These empowering skills will help you to keep moving forward in a clear and motivated manner. You're now ready to go deeper and explore and change the core issues that have kept your BPD in place for so long.

Before you move on to part 4, I recommend that you go through the summary for part 3 that's available for download at http://www.newharbinger.com/42730. This summary pulls together the concepts, activities, and exercises from part 3, and it will help strengthen what you learned.

PART 4

Reconstructing Your World and Building a New You

CHAPTER 15

Getting to the Heart of the Issue

At the heart of many BPD issues is the core content that was put in place by developmental experiences, those that happened in childhood and as you grew up. Core content influences how you see, feel, think, and react when you feel stressed, depressed, anxious, elated, abandoned, prideful, threatened, confident, happy, trapped, scared, and so on. Not all of your core content is negative, but the negative content has contributed to the development of your BPD, and negative core content is activated when people, statements, memories, beliefs, and situations cause you to feel like you're repeating past experiences and are emotionally trapped in them. This results in a flood of intense negative emotions, confusion, and conflict that people attempt to reduce any way they can. Unfortunately, people with BPD usually default to negative beliefs, behaviors, and patterns that strengthen and maintain their BPD.

In this chapter, we'll explore your core content, including its origins and influence on your default negative beliefs, behaviors, and patterns, and then develop a strategy to reduce its influence on your life. We're going to focus on reconstructing your world and building a new you who's even more impactful and powerful, and give you the skills to help you continue to grow beyond your BPD.

Remember, if you feel triggered or overwhelmed while working on your core content, you can use the strategies you learned in the earlier parts of this workbook to cope. Stop if you need to, and get the help you need. Do this work at your own pace, and only when you feel ready.

Identifying Your Core Content

Your core content is rooted in your past, and to identify it you have to think about past experiences that had a significant impact on how you see yourself, others, and the world around you. These significant early experiences usually have strong emotions attached to them, and that's what makes them so powerful. You'll use these attached emotions to identify and label your core content. Doing so will increase your awareness and help you learn how to control and contain it.

First, let's look at Tony and some of his core content so you can see how he did it.

My early experience: *My mom always paid more attention to her boyfriends and alcohol than she did to me. She put them first, whether I needed help with homework, a ride to practice, or anything else. She would tell me what a mistake I was, what a failure I was, and how I just took up space.*

This experience makes me feel (core content): *Worthless, invisible*

Tony has memories of his mother saying hurtful things to him, neglecting him, and judging him harshly. These memories created feelings of worthlessness and of being invisible, core content that still affects Tony today. But this isn't Tony's entire core content. He also had developmental experiences with teachers and coaches who believed in him and encouraged him to achieve goals. These experiences created a sense of *ability* and *determination,* positive core content areas that also influence how he feels about himself and sees the world today.

So, Tony's complete core content comprises worthlessness, feeling invisible, ability, and determination. You may be thinking, *How can you have conflicting core content? How can you feel worthless and invisible, but have a sense of ability and determination?* Great questions. Many individuals—and you may feel this way too—who have been diagnosed with BPD experience internal conflict and confusion, which is core content trying to make sense of itself. Your BPD is rooted in your confusion and conflict, and to loosen its grip and grow beyond it, you have to reduce the conflict and clear the confusion.

The first step is to find the link between your core content and early experiences. Using the following exercise, try to pinpoint no more than five core content areas, and then use one or two words to sum each up, just as Tony did. This will likely be a unique experience for you, so be patient, take a break if you need to, and come back to the exercise when you feel ready. It's perfectly normal for this exercise to take some time to complete. You can download a copy of this worksheet at http://www.newharbinger.com/42730.

My early experience: _____

_____

_____

This experience makes me feel (core content):

My early experience: _____

_____

This experience makes me feel (core content): _____

My early experience: _____

_____

_____

This experience makes me feel (core content): _____

My early experience: _____

_____

This experience makes me feel (core content): _____

My early experience: _____

_____

This experience makes me feel (core content): _____

Mapping Your Core Content Sequence

Now that you've identified your core content and its links to the past, let's look at how it drives you to respond in negative ways that disrupt how you relate to yourself, others, and situations. We'll map out the sequence, from core content activation; to intense emotion identification; to recognizing the negative beliefs, behaviors, and patterns you're driven to engage in; to short-term rewards and long-term consequences. Breaking this sequence down will help you see the driving force behind your core content, which empowers you to control it.

Let's take a look at Tony's core content sequence as an example.

When my core content areas of *worthlessness and feeling invisible* are activated, I feel (add emotions) *angry, sad, broken, confused, hopeless, and shattered.* These emotions drive me to (add beliefs, behaviors, and patterns) *drink until I pass out and try to meet someone to love, in order to feel like I have some value and importance.*

The short-term rewards are *that I feel better for a little while. I feel less alone, less broken, and I forget how hurt I feel. I forget my scars. If I do find someone, I feel like I am valued for a little while.*

The long-term consequences are *that I'm an alcoholic and healthy people don't want to be around me. I have trouble holding down a job and keeping a relationship. I just keep feeding my BPD until its stomach is full, and then it pukes me out and I'm left angry, sad, broken, confused, hopeless, and shattered all over again.*

By completing this exercise, Tony was able to identify the emotions attached to his negative core content. He saw that these emotions drove him to engage in negative beliefs, behaviors, and patterns in an effort to reduce their intensity. He was also able to see that he does these things to try and get a sense of relief and control, but they only provide short-term relief while encouraging long-term problems, such as drinking, promiscuity, and disrupted relationships.

Tony's BPD tricked him, and yours tricks you too. It makes you believe short-term relief is worth it, but the long-term cost to you, your life, and your world erases that benefit. You can live differently. You can break this sequence, reducing the effects of your core content while also learning to use adaptive and healthy beliefs, behaviors, and patterns. Be patient with yourself while completing this exercise. Take your time, and if it becomes too much, stop, take a break, seek help if you need to, and come back to it when you're ready. You can download a copy of this worksheet at http://www.newha

rbinger.com/42730. You may need to try several times before your sequence becomes clear.

When my core content areas of _____ are activated, I feel (add emotions) _____.

These emotions drive me to (add beliefs, behaviors, and patterns) _____

_____

_____

The short-term rewards are _____

_____

_____

The long-term consequences are _____

_____

Now that you've explored the origins and costs of your core content, you're ready to learn strategies to control and reduce its influence.

Controlling and Reducing Core Content

It only takes seconds to go from core content activation to negative beliefs, behaviors, and patterns. Because this transition occurs so quickly, you may believe that it's impossible to control, but that's not true. Your BPD wants you to believe this so you'll continue to seek out the reward of temporary relief by engaging in negative beliefs, behaviors, and patterns.

One way to reduce and control negative content is to use countermeasures. Typically, a *countermeasure* is an action to prevent or weaken a danger or threat. For our purposes, a countermeasure is information you can use to oppose your negative core content. Tony's core content is rooted in childhood experiences with his mother. She said hurtful things to him, making him feel worthless, and she neglected him, his interests, and his successes, making him feel invisible. To challenge his core content, Tony had to identify information proving his negative core content was wrong—his countermeasures.

My core content: *Worthlessness*

Information, or countermeasures, proving this core content is false:

1. *I was the first in my family to graduate from college, and I received many job offers.*

2. *Coaches and colleges recruited me for my baseball-playing abilities.*

3. _____

My core content: *Feeling invisible*

Information, or countermeasures, proving this core content is false:

1. *My friends come to me for support and encouragement, and they help me when I ask for it.*

2. *In relationships, I am caring, present, and kind.*

3. *My coworkers notice the good work I do and recognize my computer skills.*

Now it's your turn. If you have trouble identifying countermeasures, think about the positive things people say about you, the positive and strengthening experiences you've had, and the challenges you've overcome that prove your negative core content is wrong. This exercise may feel odd or challenging, and that's understandable. If it feels false, that's your BPD trying to trick you into believing only negative things about yourself. You can download a copy of this worksheet and the following one in the summary for part 4 at http://www.newharbinger.com/427 30.

Countermeasures to Negative Core Content

My core content: _____
Information, or countermeasures, proving this core content is false:

1. _____
2. _____
3. _____

My core content: _____
Information, or countermeasures, proving this core content is false:

1. _____
2. _____
3. _____

Your BPD wants you to believe that all core content is negative, but that's not true. BPD distorts how you see yourself, others, and situations, and, in turn, this distortion influences how you see and interpret your core content. We'll examine this distortion in more detail in the next chapter, but for now it's important for you to be aware that core content can be both negative and positive, and that breaking this content down into its components, to counter the negative and support the positive, will help you gain control over your BPD. One way to bolster positive core content is to use *supportive evidence,* information that proves your positive core content is correct. When Tony explored his positive core content without the distortion of BPD, he uncovered supportive evidence for two areas of his core content.

My positive core content: *Ability*
Supportive evidence:
1. *I have the intelligence to reason out how to get my needs met.*
2. *I'm able to complete many complicated tasks with few mistakes.*
3. *I can solve almost any puzzle or math problem.*

My core content: *Determination*
Supportive evidence:

1. *Once my goals are defined, I plan them out and I do not allow myself to be deterred.*

2. *I refuse to fail. I do not give up, like with college, baseball, and work.*

3. _____

Now it's your turn to identify supportive evidence for your positive core content. As always, take your time.

Supportive Evidence of My Positive Core Content

My core content: _____

Supportive evidence:

1. _____
2. _____
3. _____

My core content: _____

Supportive evidence:

1. _____
2. _____
3. _____

Growth Scripts

Controlling and reducing negative core content is never a "one and done" exercise. Now that you've identified countermeasures for negative core content and supportive evidence for positive core content, it's time to learn a technique for promoting your wellness and personal empowerment. *Growth scripts* are reassuring statements you say to yourself to encourage positive development. Here's one of Tony's growth scripts. He recorded it on his phone in New York City, one of his favorite places:

> *When my core content of feeling worthless is activated, I know it's untrue, because I was the first in my family to graduate college, I received many job offers, and coaches and colleges recruited me for my baseball-playing abilities. I am NOT worthless. I have endless worth.*

Tony made several scripts related to each of his core content areas, and one longer one pertaining to all four. Tony played these anywhere he wanted or was able to—while walking the streets in New York City, on a business trip, on a plane, on vacation. He played them when he felt strong and confident, and he played them when he felt tired and exhausted. He played them to boost his sense of empowerment and his ability to continue growing beyond his BPD.

The following script starter can help you write your own growth scripts. Keep in mind that you don't have to record them yourself. You can ask your significant other, a friend, a therapist, or anyone who is supportive of you growing beyond your BPD to recite your scripts for you. They can be audio or video recordings, or both. The important thing is to listen to them as often as possible. Repetition will help you get the most out of them, reducing the impact of your negative core content and supporting your positive core content. You can download a copy of these scripts in the summary for part 4 at http://www.newharbinger.com/427 30.

I know that my positive core content of _____ is accurate because _____

_____

_____

When my negative core content of _____ is activated, I know it's false because _____

_____

_____

Building Blocks for the New You

Using the spaces below, pull together what you learned from this chapter so you can take this information with you.

The most helpful information I learned from this chapter:

1. _____
2. _____
3. _____

The skills that I want to practice:

1. _____

2. _____

3. _____

While going through this chapter, I was thinking _____, and it helped me to see that _____

_____

Now that you're aware of your core content and how it affects your negative and positive beliefs, behaviors, and patterns, we'll go a step further and explore how it keeps your BPD in place by distorting your view of yourself, others, and the world.

CHAPTER 16

Distortions That Keep BPD in Place

In this chapter you're going to learn about your BPD lens; how it distorts how you see yourself, others, and situations; and how it keeps your BPD in place and encourages you to maintain your negative beliefs, behaviors, and patterns. The skills you'll learn in this chapter will help you see yourself, others, and situations more authentically, which will empower you to use adaptive and healthy response patterns and to see yourself and the world in a clear and balanced way.

Your BPD Lens

When you started this workbook, your BPD was firmly in place and had sustained itself for many years using many tactics. One of these is your BPD lens, which is a distortion of how you see and interpret yourself, others, and the world. A *distortion* is the twisting or changing of something from its true form into a false or inaccurate one. Viewing things through your BPD lens is like wearing glasses that have the wrong prescription, causing you to see only the negative side of yourself and the world around you, which influences how you think and feel about yourself, others, and situations. These distortions have played a big part in the continued existence of your BPD.

Your BPD lens encourages you to use negative beliefs, behaviors, and patterns to get your needs and wants met, but doing so results in short-term rewards and long-term consequences. Nonetheless, people with BPD tend to keep viewing things through their BPD lens in order to maintain those short-term rewards, causing a continuous cycle that locks BPD in place. When you know what your BPD lens is and how it distorts your vision, you can begin to challenge these distortions—a powerful method for seeing yourself, others, and situations as they really are, a mix of positive and negative, not just negative.

Identifying Your BPD Lens

As an example of how the BPD lens works, let's take a look at Betty and her relationship with Robert.

Betty and Robert had a very intense and volatile relationship. Robert put Betty down whenever he had the chance. For example, while she was in nursing school getting her master's degree, he'd tell her how "stupid" she was since nurses didn't need, and shouldn't have, master's degrees. "They just give out pills and check blood pressure," he'd sneer.

One afternoon Betty arrived home early and found Robert online Skyping with another woman. They were laughing and joking, and when Betty walked in he started making fun of her, calling her "Nurse Einstein." The woman he was online with laughed along with him.

When Betty decided to challenge her BPD and grow beyond it, she had to take a long look at what her BPD lens was causing her to see and feel regarding herself, others, and situations.

These are the answers she gave for an exercise I had her do related to the incident above.

My BPD lens causes me to see myself as: *A failure and being lost, empty, trapped, and alone. I see how my mom makes me feel, like no one cares about me and that I'm not good enough to be a nurse or anything else. I'm stuck in "another lost and dead-end relationship," as my mom used to say.*

When I think of (name an important person in your life) *Robert,* my BPD lens causes me to see and think: *He's someone I have to have in my life or I will be all alone. I have to put up with his shit because no one else will have me. He's the best I'm going to get and I should just be happy with that. I deserve no better, so I should just take it.*

When I think of (name a situation) *him making fun of me with other women,* my BPD causes me to see and think: *I want to hurt myself, cry, and scream. I want to go off on him and make him feel like I feel. I want to just hook up with somebody—anybody—just to feel okay, even if for only a little while.*

Betty's BPD lens caused her to feel stuck within her BPD, with few options and mounting negatives. This is what your BPD wants you to believe and feel, as well, so it can continue to exist. To counter it, take some time to identify how your BPD lens influences how you see yourself, others, and the world. Write freely, holding nothing back. There are no wrong answers. You can download a copy of this worksheet at http://www.newharbinger.com/42730.

My BPD lens causes me to see myself as: _____

_____

_____

_____

When I think of (name an important person in your life) _____, my BPD lens causes me to see and think:

_____

_____

_____

When I think of (name a situation) _____, my BPD causes me to see and think: _____

In the space below, list the people (significant other, family members, boss, coworkers, friends) and situations (standing in line, a staff meeting, disciplining your child) you'd like to work on using this exercise.

You've identified how your BPD lens influences what you see, think, and feel about yourself, others, and situations. This was likely not an easy thing to do, but it was a brave thing to do, and you should give yourself credit for sticking with it.

We know that your BPD lens helped your BPD continue to thrive; kept your negative beliefs, behaviors, and patterns in place; and caused you to be reluctant to do things differently. It did this by creating a cycle of negatives, which has been at the heart of what has kept you stuck.

Your BPD Lens Cycle

Your BPD lens rewards you. If it didn't, you would've discarded it a long time ago. It keeps you vigilant, seeing only hurts and harm, which fills you with feelings of hate, fear, mistrust, abandonment, emptiness, anger, and many other distracting and overwhelming emotions. These distortions lead you to engage in your negative beliefs, behaviors, and patterns, which leads to the short-term reward of thinking and feeling like you're in control, even if only for a short time, and even if you're not actually in control. Due to the perceived rewards, the cycle created by your BPD lens continues.

Let's look at how the cycle worked in relation to Betty's relationship with Robert. Betty felt that Robert's treatment of her was justified based upon her past experiences with her mom. While growing up, her mom often went out and left her at home alone, or she was locked in her room when her mom brought men home. Betty's mom always put others first, leading Betty to feel abandoned and empty inside. These experiences fed her negative core content (abandonment and emptiness) and made her willing to give up her integrity and resolve, preventing her from seeking out something better. Her core content showed up in her relationship with Robert. She accepted abusive, neglectful, and mean treatment as the price of having someone in her life, because she was raised to believe that she deserved such treatment and should accept it.

Betty's BPD lens cycle supported her beliefs by reminding her of how painful, lonely, dangerous, and frightening the world is, and that everyone around her was a source of pain who would eventually leave her lonely and afraid. Her reward for keeping people at an emotional and physical distance, and for accepting her loneliness and how Robert treated her, was the perception of less stress and anxiety. Let's examine the rewards Betty received from her BPD lens using her answers to an exercise she completed.

If, based on my BPD lens, I see or believe *that I am all alone and no one wants to be with me because I'm so broken, bad, harmful, and unnecessary,* then (beliefs, behaviors, and patterns) *I push people away before they can abandon me and break my heart.* The benefit of doing this is that I (BPD lens short-term reward) *protect myself and I feel safe.*

If, based on my BPD lens, I see or believe *that people always hold me back and prevent me from succeeding and achieving my goals, and do nothing but lie to me,* then (beliefs, behaviors, and patterns) *I am ready to fight and defend myself for when they are going to hurt me or leave me.* The benefit of doing this is that I (BPD lens short-term reward) *hurt them before they hurt me, and I feel safe because they were going to leave me anyway.*

From Betty's examples, can you recognize the progression from seeing something through her BPD lens to her beliefs, behaviors, and patterns to her rewards? It's an "if/then" cycle. *If* Betty sees and believes these things about her world, she *then* responds in a way that leads to the short-term reward of feeling safe and in control, which causes the cycle to continue.

Let's examine your BPD lens cycle to help you recognize the perceived short-term rewards you get from it that keep it in place. You can download a copy of this worksheet at http://www.n ewharbinger.com/42730.

If, based on my BPD lens, I see or believe _____

_____

_____

then (beliefs, behaviors, and patterns) _____

_____

The benefit of doing this is that I (BPD lens short-term reward) _____

_____

If, based on my BPD lens, I see or believe _____

then (beliefs, behaviors, and patterns) _____

The benefit of doing this is that I (BPD lens short-term reward) _____

If, based on my BPD lens, I see or believe _____

then (beliefs, behaviors, and patterns) _____

The benefit of doing this is that I (BPD lens short-term reward) _____

By identifying your BPD lens cycle, you're able to see the distortion it creates, which gives you the power to break the cycle using your authentic view.

Your Authentic View

Your authentic view is about seeing the world as it really is, without distortion. Having an authentic view is like having the correct prescription for your glasses: you're able to see yourself, others, and situations clearly and accurately.

Keep in mind that your authentic view isn't all sunshine and roses. It's a balanced, realistic view of the world around you, in which negatives appear negative, and positives appear positive. This lack of sugarcoating allows you to address your core content honestly, so you can strengthen the positive and minimize or extinguish the negative.

Like all skills, breaking your BPD lens and building your authentic view takes time and practice. Practice the skills you're about to learn as often as you can. You'll find that you're more empowered, receive more short-term and long-term rewards, and have better relationships with yourself and others.

Identifying Your Authentic View

Your authentic view will be based upon balance, and when you're balanced you feel calm, collected, and clear, as opposed to when you're using your BPD lens, which causes you to be unbalanced and fills you with negative thoughts and feelings. Because you've been using your BPD lens for so long, identifying and strengthening your authentic view may seem daunting, so let's start this exercise by looking at Betty's authentic view.

If I'm using my authentic view, then I feel relaxed and calm. I can concentrate, and my thoughts are at a pace slow enough for me to understand them. If I feel less stress about the future then I am aware of where I am and how I feel at this moment. If I feel my breath go in and out, and it's under my control, then I can see the situation I am in clearly, and I can balance my thoughts to determine the best outcome for me.

These were very empowering thoughts and feelings for Betty. Because her authentic view reduced or removed the distortion, conflict, and confusion associated with her BPD, she could choose to respond to people and situations differently using the adaptive and healthy patterns she developed in part 3 of the workbook. When she started using these, she was able to see that her wants and needs could be met, and that she didn't have to hurt or harm herself or others, increasing the likelihood that she'd receive both short-term and long-term rewards.

Now it's your turn to describe your authentic view. To help you identify a calm, collected, and clear state, follow these relaxation steps:

1.   Find a quiet, comfortable place to sit or lie down.
2.   Take a typical breath, followed by a deep breath. Breathe in slowly through your nose, allowing your chest and lower belly to rise as you fill your lungs. Let your belly fully expand.
3.   Slowly breathe out through your mouth or nose—whatever feels

natural. Do this a few times, until you feel calm, collected, and clear.

Now just write what comes to mind when you imagine yourself feeling calm, collected, and clear. Don't hold back. If your BPD lens starts to interfere with negative, stressful, and distorting thoughts, images, and beliefs, imagine them on a greasy floor slipping right out the door of your mind. Allow only thoughts that promote calm, collected, and clear thinking to stick around. If you have trouble finding this balance, give the mindfulness technique you learned in chapter 13 a try, or any of the others you learned. After you've written out your authentic view, take a few moments to examine the experience by answering the prompts that follow.

If I'm using my authentic view, *then*

_____

_____

_____

Describe what it was like mentally (thoughts and images), emotionally (feelings), and physically (body sensations, such as a slowed heart rate) when you reached a calm, collected, and clear state.

_____
_____
_____

Describe what you learned about yourself (the power of your authentic view, the strength of your personal control, and so on) having identified your authentic view.

_____
_____
_____

Now that you've identified and explored your authentic view, let's go over ways to enhance it so you have even greater control over how you see the world and react to it.

Enhancing Your Authentic View

This exercise will increase your understanding of your authentic view and its effect on how you see yourself, others, and situations. This knowledge will enhance your ability to recognize and resist the urge to go back to seeing yourself, others, and the world through your BPD lens.

As you complete the exercise, be aware that your BPD lens may try to interfere, and remember that your authentic view is based upon you feeling and thinking in a calm, collected, and clear manner. Enhancing your authentic view may require coming to terms with aspects of yourself you don't like, recognizing things about others that aren't good for you that you don't want to see, and identifying situations in the past when you had choices but it was easier to believe you had none. These are not easy tasks, but they're important ones to help you continue on this journey of growth beyond your BPD. Do your best, and resist allowing your BPD to trigger you.

Just like with previous exercises, be patient with yourself. You're learning a new skill and a new way to see the world, so go at your own pace. If this exercise brings up too many thoughts, images, and beliefs, and you start to feel overwhelmed, stop, take a break, and consult a healthy friend or mental health provider and return to it when you're ready.

When I look at myself using my authentic view, I see, feel, and think:

_____

When I think of (name an important person in your life) _____ using my authentic view, I see, feel, and think:

_____

When I see, feel, and think of (name a situation, such as an argument, being at work, being talked down to) _____ using my authentic view, I see, feel, and think:

_____

_____

Now that you've identified your authentic view and the way it influences how you see yourself, others, and situations, you can generate your authentic view cycle. This cycle supports positive beliefs, behaviors, and patterns and encourages healthy connections with yourself and others.

Your Authentic View Cycle

Just like your BPD lens, your authentic view has a cycle as well. When you see yourself, others, and the world through your authentic view, you're able to see your true talents and power, as well as all the options you have for being a positive force in your life. This, in turn, increases the likelihood of you receiving positive short-term *and* long-term rewards. This cycle is very rewarding, which causes you to continue seeing the world with your authentic view. Before we identify your cycle, let's take a look at Betty's experience as she removed her BPD lens and used her authentic view in her relationship with Robert.

If I use my authentic view, then I see *that Robert is mean to me, doesn't respect me, and is unkind, unfaithful, and abusive. I see that he talks to other women online, doesn't help with the bills or with cleaning the house, and makes me feel like my mom made me feel.*

If I believe these things, then (authentic view rewards) *I know I have to make changes. I see that I don't deserve to be treated this way and that I can meet someone who will be kind, caring, and respectful. I am smart, skilled, strong, and worthwhile. I know I have options.*

Using her authentic view, Betty recognized that she's smart, skilled, strong, and worthwhile. She determined that she was the best person that Robert had ever been with, and she knew that the abuse had gone on long enough. Knowing all of this, she put a plan in place to separate from Robert and move on. She felt powerful, in control, and able to make positive changes. Her authentic view rewarded her with good feelings and good results, and thus she wanted to use it more often and in many other situations.

Do you see how the authentic view cycle follows an "if/then" sequence? *If* Betty sees the world using her authentic view, and she believes what she sees and acts accordingly, she *then* is rewarded with a positive view of herself, which encourages her to go out and get positive things she deserves, such as a boyfriend who is kind and caring. This cycle can work the same way for you. The opposite is also true: when you see the world through your BPD lens, a negative cycle is promoted. Now it's your turn to examine your authentic view cycle, so you can see the rewards you get from using it. You can download a copy of this worksheet at http://www.newharbinger.com/42730.

If I use my authentic view, then I see _____

_____

If I believe these things, then (authentic view rewards) _____

_____

If I use my authentic view, then I see _____

_____

If I believe these things, then (authentic view rewards) _____

Many people feel empowered by their authentic view and the cycle it creates, but also a little scared. This is a normal reaction, as trying new things can be intimidating. You've been seeing the world through your BPD lens for a long time, but that time is coming to an end, and a new perspective is emerging—along with a new you.

The skills you're learning take practice and patience, and like building any skill, the more you use it, the easier it becomes. Use your authentic view cycle when you're having difficulty communicating with your significant other, a family member, or your children. Try it out when you're in a frustrating or triggering situation at work or with friends. Redo the exercises in this chapter over and over again, whenever you need to. Using your authentic view is a skill that will build your sense of self-control and personal power. It's a major piece of this journey to grow beyond your BPD.

Building Blocks for the New You

Using the spaces below, pull together what you learned from this chapter so you can take this information with you.

The most helpful information I learned from this chapter:

1. _____
2. _____
3. _____

The skills that I want to practice:

1. _____
2. _____
3. _____

While going through this chapter, I was thinking _____, and it helped me to see that _____
_____
_____

Now that you're beginning to see the world without your BPD lens, it's time to address the destructive fears, beliefs, and wishes that have been holding you back.

CHAPTER 17

Growing Beyond Destructive Fears, Beliefs, and Wishes

Destructive fears, beliefs, and wishes are based on negative emotions, such as hate and anxiety, that support or encourage negative thinking, such as that you deserve to be broken and harmed and that the world is full of pain and loneliness. These destructive emotions were created right along with your BPD and your core content, and they're usually linked to people in your life who were involved in the negative experiences that generated your core content. Destructive fears, beliefs, and wishes, along with your negative core content and your BPD lens, keep your BPD in place by supporting negative beliefs, behaviors, and patterns. They cause you problems in relationships and in the situations you find yourself in every day, leaving you with short-term rewards and long-term consequences. This chapter is going to help you identify, uncover, challenge, and change them.

Recognizing Your Identified Others

Many of the destructive fears, beliefs, and wishes you hold stem from interactions you had with people you were close to. These individuals played a critical role in the experiences you had growing up, particularly those that related to the creation of your core content and the distortions that affect how you see the world. I use the term "identified others" for these folks, because for most people more than one individual influenced their growth and development and had a role in the creation of their BPD. That said, you may only have one identified other, and that's fine.

Your identified others are very powerful figures because, as you grew up, you made them a part of you. It's like their feelings, beliefs, values, expectations, and so on are inside of you, which influences how you treat yourself and others and react in situations. Due to this, it's not uncommon to feel anger, rage, resentment, and hostility toward these identified others, as well as love, caring, and desire for them. These conflicting emotions create confusion, which we know is a key part of how your BPD keeps itself in place.

Tony reflected on his early experiences and related core content to pinpoint his identified others.

My early experience: *Mom paid more attention to her boyfriends and alcohol than she did to me. She always ignored me and neglected me when her boyfriends wanted something, and they always wanted something. She didn't come to my baseball games or college graduation. She didn't even help me pick out a college because she wanted to get drunk and be with them instead.*

Core content: *Worthlessness, feeling invisible*

My identified others: *Mom*

It may look like Tony only had one early experience, but it's something that happened over and over while he was growing up. This is typical of the early experiences that create our core content. Tony could've listed other significant life experiences involving past girlfriends, coaches, friends, coworkers, and others who helped create his BPD, but he chose the person he felt was most influential.

Tony carries this early experience and these core content areas (worthlessness and feeling invisible) with him, and they influence his negative beliefs, behaviors, and patterns. They cause him to *fear* doing things differently; encourage his *belief* in a negative, harmful, and hurtful present and future; and are the foundation of the destructive *wish* he has to fulfill the expectation of failure and neglect he learned from his mother to gain her attention, love, approval, forgiveness, respect, and admiration. After identifying this early experience and the related core content, Tony was able to name his identified other: his mom. Now it's your turn.

This exercise is meant to help you recognize the identified others who are connected to your early experiences and related core content. You'll first describe a memorable early experience with as much detail as you feel comfortable providing. The experience should be something you went through or witnessed while you were growing up that has stuck with you and affects how you see the world. Then, you'll identify the associated core content, and, finally, the person, or people—your identified others—who were important parts of the experience. Perhaps these identified others caused the experience, made the experience worse, or influenced how you felt about the experience. If you find yourself stuck or in need of assistance, don't forget the HELP steps from the book's introduction. Use extra paper if you need to, or you can download a copy of this worksheet at http://www.n ewharbinger.com/42730.

My early experience: _____
_____
_____

Core content: _____
My identified others: _____
My early experience: _____

Core content: _____
My identified others: _____
My early experience: _____

_____

Core content: _____
My identified others: _____

Now that you've linked early experiences, core content, and identified others, let's take the next step and reveal the related destructive fears, beliefs, and wishes.

Uncovering Your Destructive Fears, Beliefs, and Wishes

Your BPD has distorted the way in which you try to obtain the love, approval, forgiveness, respect, admiration, and attention you want and deserve. It does this by leading you to believe that you can get this sense of fulfillment and satisfaction through negative beliefs, behaviors, and patterns, which leave you with short-term rewards but without long-term stability, happiness, and growth. You can reverse this trend.

Let's first return to the example of Tony and his mother and take a look at an exercise he did to develop a deeper understanding of his destructive fears, beliefs, and wishes.

My identified others: *Mom*

My early experience: *Mom paid more attention to her boyfriends and alcohol than she did to me. She always ignored me and neglected me when her boyfriends wanted something, and they always wanted something. She didn't come to my baseball games or college graduation. She didn't even help me pick out a college because she wanted to get drunk and be with them instead.*

This experience led to my core content of *worthlessness and feeling invisible,* which causes me to *fear* that *no one will notice me or recognize all that I have done and achieved. I will be worthless and invisible to the world.*

These fears cause me to *believe* that *no one cares about me, that I am second to everyone else. People in my life always choose someone else over me. I'm unable to achieve what I need to achieve but I don't know what that is, so I just float through my life.*

These beliefs cause me to wish that all of her men would leave her and take everything she has, causing her to suffer enough to recognize that I am here and have value, purpose, and gifts.

Tony's responses really brought his fears, beliefs, and wishes to light, which helped him address them and control them better. Tony's revenge-like fantasy for his mom is not an uncommon wish, and you may have similar wishes for your identified others as well. Many people want to inflict pain or exact revenge upon their identified others or punish or torture them in some manner. It's normal to have these thoughts and feelings, but it's important to get these out of the dark and into the light, where you can determine how they impact you and your behavior.

It's your turn to uncover your destructive fears, beliefs, and wishes and the influence they have on you. Consider these exploration prompts as you identify them:

Fears

- I am afraid that my identified others will...
- I fear that ... will happen if...
- I fear that my identified others will ... if I don't...

Beliefs

- I believe that my identified others think ... about me.
- When I think about my identified others and how they think of me, I believe they...
- Based on my experiences with my identified others, I believe...

Wishes

- When I think about my identified others, I wish...
- I wish my identified others would...
- My wish is for my identified others to think, feel, recognize, or experience...

Remember, do the best you can and don't rush this exercise. There are no right or wrong answers. Don't forget the HELP steps, if you need them. Use extra paper if you need to, or you can download a copy of this worksheet at http://www.newharbinger.com/42730.

My identified others: _____
My early experience: _____

_____

_____

This experience led to my core content of _____, which causes me to *fear* that _____

_____

These fears cause me to *believe* that _____

_____

These beliefs cause me to *wish* that _____

_____

By uncovering your destructive fears, beliefs, and wishes you're now ready to go forward and challenge them by exploring their place in your past, present, and future.

Challenging Your Destructive Fears, Beliefs, and Wishes

Challenging and growing beyond your destructive fears, beliefs, and wishes starts with identifying where they have had the greatest influence on you, and then developing a vision for how your life will look and feel without them. It also involves becoming comfortable with your new adaptive and healthy beliefs, behaviors, and patterns.

Take your time with this exercise, but don't overthink your answers. Let your thoughts flow after reading the prompts, and encourage yourself to explore your fear, beliefs, and wishes free of the destructive influence of your BPD. It may be helpful to do this exercise over and over again as you continue to grow beyond your BPD, so you can download a blank copy of it in the summary for part 4 at http://www .newharbinger.com/42730. I included examples of Tony's responses first.

My identified others, early experiences, and core content helped create my destructive fears, beliefs, and wishes by *making me feel like I had no choice but to follow the path of my BPD, which led me to hurt myself, others, and opportunities I had. I lived my life based on the fear of not being good enough, on the belief I would lose everything, and with the wish that my BPD would get me all the love and caring I always wanted, but it didn't.*

My destructive fears, beliefs, and wishes hold me back by *causing me to believe my mother, which drives overwhelming, yet familiar and comfortable, uneasiness, fear, confusion, and conflict that push me to drink, cheat on my girlfriend, and destroy all I have built for myself.*

My destructive fears, beliefs, and wishes cause me to inflict self-damage by *defaulting to the negative beliefs, behaviors, and patterns of drinking and sleeping around, chasing women to get some, or any, sense of being recognized. I push my ability and determination to the side and wallow in my pain and wait for someone to save me from my worthlessness and feelings of being invisible, but only negative people come into my life, and they don't really want to save me. Instead they just amplify my mother's thoughts about me, and my feelings of being alone, sad, and worthless. I am a master at self-destruction.*

Without my destructive fears, beliefs, and wishes, I see my life being more honest. I see myself being able to recognize both the good and the bad in the people in my life, and that the things people say and do don't have to impact me, if I don't want them to. I'm able to understand my emotions better and to control myself without feeling pushed or manipulated by my identified other—my mother. I'm in control.

My life is good right now because I have a relationship with someone I can feel close to and I know she respects me. I know my boundaries with her and she knows her boundaries with me. I can feel appreciated at my job when I do a good job and get things right, and this causes me to have an awesome day.

Without my destructive fears, beliefs, and wishes, I'm able to be myself, see my life without my BPD lens—that it has possibilities—and control myself by using my mindfulness skills. I can control my button responses and triggers because I'm not stuck in my old cycle of patterns and self-hatred.

Now that you've seen Tony's responses, take some time and answer the prompts on your own.

My identified others, early experiences, and core content helped create my destructive fears, beliefs, and wishes by _____

_____

_____

_____

My destructive fears, beliefs, and wishes hold me back by _____

_____

_____

_____

My destructive fears, beliefs, and wishes cause me to inflict self-damage by _____

_____

_____

Without my destructive fears, beliefs, and wishes, I see my life being _____

My life is good right now because
_____

Without my destructive fears, beliefs, and wishes, I'm able to _____

Strengthening Adaptive and Healthy Hopes, Beliefs, and Wishes

Now that you've challenged your destructive fears, beliefs, and wishes, you're ready to identify and embody adaptive and healthy hopes, beliefs, and wishes. These will move you forward; bring you peace, confidence, and clarity; and help you openly and honestly get the love, approval, forgiveness, respect, admiration, and attention you want and deserve. With time and work, you'll be able to replace those old destructive BPD patterns with new adaptive and healthy ones.

The first step in this exercise is to briefly explore an example of positive core content you identified in chapter 15. You can download a copy of this exercise at http://www.newharbin ger.c om/42730.

My positive core content: _____

My positive core content gives me hope that I can _____

_____

_____

My positive core content causes me to believe that _____

_____

_____

My positive core content causes me to wish that _____

_____

_____

Positive core content is powerful. It can help you replace your destructive fears, beliefs, and wishes with healthy hopes, beliefs, and wishes. Take a few moments to complete the prompts below.

I know my future has hope because _____

_____

I have greater control over my thoughts, feelings, and behaviors when _____

_____

_____

To reach a state of peace, calmness, confidence, and clarity I will _____

_____

I can be kind to myself by _____

_____

I can be kind to others by _____

_____

With my adaptive and healthy hopes, beliefs, and wishes I can _____

Reminding yourself of this positive content routinely can strengthen your confidence in a future full of both short-term and long-term rewards, as well as stability inside yourself and with others.

Building Blocks for the New You

Using the spaces below, pull together what you learned from this chapter so you can take this information with you.

The most helpful information I learned from this chapter:

1. _____
2. _____
3. _____

The skills that I want to practice:

1. _____
2. _____
3. _____

While going through this chapter, I was thinking _____, and it helped me to see that _____

Now that you're growing beyond your destructive fears, beliefs, and wishes with healthy hopes, beliefs, and wishes, it's time to address the defense mechanisms that have been holding you back.

CHAPTER 18

Defense Mechanisms and Healthy Coping and Responding

In this chapter you're going to identify the unhealthy defense mechanisms that keep your BPD in place and replace them with healthy and adaptive defense mechanisms to enhance your ability to cope with and respond to difficult people and situations more effectively.

What Are Defense Mechanisms?

Defense mechanisms are psychological tools that help us get our needs met and keep our core content safe. They influence how we see, interpret, and react to the world around us and the people within it. We all use them. The defense mechanisms you use, when you use them, and with whom are directly linked to your core content, BPD lens, identified others, and adaptive and healthy hopes, beliefs, and wishes.

Most people are aware of unhealthy defense mechanisms, which are also called pathological, immature, or neurotic defenses. These are learned responses that exist in young children, adolescents, and adults. Even though these mechanisms keep us, and our core content, psychologically safe, so we're not overwhelmed by feelings, thoughts, and experiences we're not prepared to handle, they can interfere with our ability to accurately interpret reality, maintain and build relationships, and lead fulfilling lives.

Not all defense mechanisms are unhealthy; in fact, there are healthy ones that can help you understand, interpret, and respond to the fear, pain, confusion, and conflict associated with your BPD. Healthy defense mechanisms, also called mature defenses, can improve your sense of fulfillment, pleasure, and self-control by helping you to positively evaluate and process conflicting feelings, thoughts, and experiences. Let's take a closer look at unhealthy and healthy defense mechanisms.

Unhealthy Defense Mechanisms

Nine unhealthy defense mechanisms have been found to be most prevalent in individuals with BPD (Perry, Presniak, and Olson 2013).

Unhealthy Defense Mechanism	Definition and Example
Acting out	This involves acting on impulse to avoid a feeling, belief, thought, or image rather than waiting for a more appropriate time to deal with it. By acting out, you avoid the frustration and anxiety of postponing a particular behavior. For example, Betty pushed her coworker when she felt disrespected at work.
Denial	This involves rejecting the reality of a feeling, belief, thought, or image. Denial prevents you from recognizing negative or uncomfortable information about yourself, others, or situations. For example, Betty denied that cutting herself caused people who cared about her to worry.
Devaluation/ idealization	This involves seeing another person or situation as extremely negative, which causes you to only recognize bad feelings, beliefs, thoughts, or images. Minutes, hours, or days later you may see the same person or situation as extremely positive, causing you to only recognize good feelings, beliefs, thoughts, or images. For example, Betty thought her new psychologist was wonderful and brilliant, but days later she called him "the devil" and concluded he was ignorant.
Intellectualization	This involves avoiding a feeling, belief, thought, or image by using information and data only. For example, Betty refused to practice safe sex because she "only had" a 1 in 1,250 chance of getting HIV from unprotected sex when she acted out promiscuously (Boily et al. 2009).
Passive aggression	This involves indirectly expressing frustration or anger by failing on purpose, procrastinating, faking an illness, and so on. It causes others difficulty, anger, or frustration. For example, because Betty didn't like her boss, she purposefully turned a report in late so her boss would get into trouble.
Projection	This involves thinking someone else has your feelings, beliefs, thoughts, or images. For example, Betty hated her boss, but that feeling was overwhelming for her, so she believed her boss hated her instead.

Rationalization	This involves generating various explanations to justify actions or the situation you're in while denying your feelings. For example, Betty told herself that it was okay to cheat on Robert because he cheated on her.
Repression	This involves pushing distressing feelings, impulses, ideas, or wishes out of awareness. For example, Betty can't remember when her dad left her family because the memory is too painful.
Splitting self and others	This involves seeing yourself, or others, as all good or all bad as opposed to a mixture of positive and negative attributes. The shifts can be rapid and intense. For example, Betty thought her friend Tammy was a terrible person because she forgot to call her before she went out one night.

As you went through the list, did some of these unhealthy defense mechanisms seem like your go-to responses or coping strategies? Can you think of certain people with whom you use unhealthy defense mechanisms, or situations in which you employ them? Before we explore these important questions further, let's examine Betty's defense mechanisms (in parentheses) in the following example.

The argument began after Betty arrived home late, having worked a fourteen-hour shift at the hospital. Her boyfriend, Michael, calmly and clearly asked her, "What happened at work? How come you're late?"

Betty was tired and felt attacked. She thought Michael was accusing her of being dishonest and unfaithful, and she said, "I'm tired and I don't have to justify myself to you! You're not my daddy! Who do you think you are?" (Acting out, projection, rationalization, splitting self and others)

Michael raised his voice and said, "Here we go again, causing problems when there aren't any! Just shut it down already!" The argument grew in intensity from there.

Betty yelled back, "You shit-heel! You don't know a thing about what I go through each day, and you just don't care!" (Acting out, rationalization, splitting self and others) Michael's guard went up, and he yelled, "Why are you jumping all over me! I didn't even do anything wrong!" He continued cussing and refused to admit he'd made a mistake.

Betty responded with her default negative response pattern involving yelling, cussing, name-calling, refusing to apologize, and seeing only one side of the story (acting out, denial, projection, rationalization, splitting self and others). Betty grew more upset and threw books at him, followed by the TV remote (acting out). She started to think that Michael was going to rush out of the house and leave her forever, and a feeling of emptiness began to build inside of her. The argument continued until Betty ran into the bathroom and cut herself (acting out), while Michael beat on the door for her to come out.

Betty didn't use all nine unhealthy defense mechanisms, and you may not either. She tended to engage in acting out, denial, projection, rationalization, and splitting self and others. The defense mechanisms you use may depend on the person you're with and the situation you're in. Before we identify your unhealthy defense mechanisms, let's go over healthy defense mechanisms, so you can be sure you're exploring every angle.

Healthy Defense Mechanisms

Most people, including people with BPD, don't use only unhealthy defense mechanisms to manage fear, pain, confusion, and conflict. They also use healthy defense mechanisms, which improve their sense of fulfillment, pleasure, and self-control. There are six healthy defense mechanisms listed here that can help you positively evaluate and process conflicting feelings, thoughts, and experiences.

Healthy Defense Mechanism	Definition and Example
Altruism	This involves experiencing pleasure or managing pain by helping others, with little or no thought of how it will benefit you. For example, Betty volunteered at the local animal shelter after her cat passed away.
Anticipation	This involves planning for future stress, fear, and discomfort and exploring a desired outcome and the probability of success or failure. For example, Betty noticed that nurse's shifts were getting cut at the hospital. Seeing the trend in cutbacks, with the knowledge that she had been one of the most recent nurses hired, she began to search for jobs so she'd be aware of her options if the hospital let her go, or if her hours were cut.
Humor	This involves openly expressing feelings and thoughts in an amusing or comedic way without causing others pain or discomfort (such as through sarcasm or humor at another's expense). One's wit can lessen uncomfortable thoughts, feelings, and beliefs. For example, Betty treated a patient with cancer who joked about being bald after going through chemotherapy.

Self-discipline	This involves controlling or removing the pleasurable effects of short-term rewards, which come from negative beliefs, behaviors, and patterns. With self-discipline you determine what is best for you and feel satisfied when you finally renounce blatant and hurtful pleasures. For example, Betty committed to changing herself and her life by seeking help and overcoming her BPD.
Sublimation	This involves being capable of meeting goals by using skills to reduce stress rather than increasing it or blocking it out. Sublimation leads to feelings of gratification. For example, Betty felt intense anger toward her mother, friends, and boyfriends that she redirected into working out.
Suppression	This involves making the choice to avoid thinking about something negative or delaying the impulse to respond. For example, Betty really liked Michael and wanted to be in a relationship with him, but she made the choice to take her time and get to know him first before jumping in.

Were you able to identify the healthy defense mechanisms you use? Let's turn again to Betty's argument with Michael, this time looking at it through the lens of healthy defense mechanisms.

Betty came home from working a fourteen-hour shift at the hospital. She recognized that she was tired because she'd stayed an extra two hours to deal with a patient emergency (altruism). As she pulled into the driveway she took a deep breath and remembered that she hadn't called Michael, realizing that he was probably worried about her (anticipation, self-discipline, suppression). She walked into the house and Michael calmly and clearly asked, "What happened at work? How come you're late?"

Betty took a deep breath, recognized his statement of concern and compassion, remembered that she didn't have to prove anything, pushed her guilt out of her mind, and responded, "I'm sorry. I totally forgot to call you" (sublimation, suppression). "A patient had a seizure, and a member of the treatment team had called in sick, so I stayed until we could get the situation under control" (altruism, sublimation).

Michael paused for a moment, looking at her from the couch. "I know you work a lot and that you give a lot to your job, but when you don't call me I worry that you might be hurt. Please try to call next time, and I'm glad you're okay."

Betty was able to get a sense of fulfillment, pleasure, and self-control by effectively evaluating and processing her feelings, thoughts, and experiences using anticipation, self-discipline, sublimation, and suppression. She used healthy defense mechanisms to achieve a positive outcome and to strengthen her relationship with someone she cared about very much.

Let's now take a look at the healthy and unhealthy defense mechanisms you use. In the spaces below, list those you've identified from the lists.

Healthy Defense Mechanisms	Unhealthy Defense Mechanisms

Don't worry if you use more unhealthy defense mechanisms than healthy ones. The objective is to recognize the ones you tend to use in response to yourself, others, and situations, topics we'll explore next.

People, Situations, and Defense Mechanisms

Which defense mechanisms you tend to use is related to the people you're with, the situation you're in, and the feelings, thoughts, and memories you're having at the time. You probably use some defense mechanisms more than others. Increasing our awareness of the defense mechanisms we tend to use can help us understand and control them. Betty used the following worksheet to explore her defense mechanisms—both healthy and unhealthy ones.

People, Situations, and Defense Mechanisms Record

I tend to use (defense mechanism) *acting out* with *my friends, Robert, mom, and people I work with* because *I want to control the situation or I just can't wait any longer for them to do what I want them to do. I use acting out to make sure that I'm noticed, so I won't disappear and vanish into nothingness. Acting out gives me a rush, making me feel like I'm alive and present, because when things get too slow I get scared that people won't like me because I'm boring and dull. I use acting out when I get "itchy," when I'm alone, or when I'm feeling abandoned and empty.*

I tend to use (defense mechanism) suppression with Michael and doctors at work because I'm better able to control myself and to build up my relationships with them. Michael is patient and caring with me, when I let him be, and his kindness causes me to fear that he'll abandon me and I'll be left with an empty hole inside. I'm determined to improve this relationship, and suppression gives me the permission to decide what is best for me. I can see the steps I need to take to help Michael, myself, and our relationship. I use suppression with the doctors at the hospital when it seems like they're talking down to me. I consider this the best response and course of action, so

I'm able to keep the job I love and get to continue to take care of patients.

In both examples Betty identified the defense mechanism she used, the people she used it with most often, the situations she used it in, and how she benefited from using it. This information about herself gave her a greater understanding of her unhealthy and healthy defense mechanisms, as well as more control of when, where, and with whom she used them.

Now it's your turn to identify yours. Don't rush through this exercise. If you need to take a break, allow yourself that time away, and then return to the worksheet when you feel ready to reengage. You can download a copy of it at http://www.newharbinger.com/427 30.

People, Situations, and Defense Mechanisms Record

I tend to use (defense mechanism)

_____

with _____ because _____

_____

_____

I tend to use (defense mechanism)
with _____ because _____

_____

_____

I tend to use (defense mechanism)
with _____ because _____

_____

_____

I tend to use (defense mechanism)
_____

with _____ because _____

_____

_____

You've gained a lot of valuable information about yourself, your unhealthy and healthy defense mechanisms, and the situations and people that affect their use. Let's dive a little deeper into the topic, looking at how defense mechanisms keep your core content safe. This exploration should help you see the benefits of using healthy defense mechanisms.

From Core Content and Defense Mechanisms to Positive Outcomes

Utilizing healthy defense mechanisms instead of unhealthy ones requires reworking the process you go through once your core content is activated. The process from the activating event to engaging in unhealthy or healthy defense mechanisms can literally take milliseconds, but over time and with continued use it has come to feel automatic. When you understand and slow down this sequence, you're empowered with choice regarding how you act toward others and react in many situations.

To gain this control, it helps to track your process using the Defense Mechanisms Outcome Log, on which you identify the event that activated your core content, the defense mechanism you used, and the positive or negative outcome. This exercise can help you see the benefit of using healthy defense mechanisms over unhealthy ones, because the former significantly increases the likelihood of a positive outcome. As you use healthy defense mechanisms more, they will become automatic adaptive and healthy response patterns.

Here are two examples from Betty. For simplification, I separated the healthy and unhealthy examples, but in reality you're likely to use both types of defense mechanisms in the same situation or with the same individual. When you fill out your own log, keep this in mind.

Defense Mechanisms Outcome Log

My core content of *abandonment, integrity, and resolve* was activated when *I knew I was late and hadn't called Michael, and he asked me where I'd been.*

I used the following defense mechanisms (circle all the ones you used).

Unhealthy Defense Mechanisms	Healthy Defense Mechanisms
Acting out	Altruism
Denial	Anticipation
Devaluation/idealization	Humor
Intellectualization	Self-discipline
Passive aggression	Sublimation
Projection	Suppression
Rationalization	
Repression	
Splitting self and others	

The outcome of the situation: *Michael and I got into it. I started screaming, and he started screaming. I cussed and threw things at him until I got so overwhelmed that I ran into the bathroom and cut myself while Michael beat on the door for me to come out.*

My core content of *abandonment, integrity, and resolve* was activated when *I knew I was late and hadn't called Michael, and he asked me where I'd been.*

I used the following defense mechanisms (circle all the ones you used).

Unhealthy Defense Mechanisms	Healthy Defense Mechanisms
Acting out	Altruism
Denial	Anticipation
Devaluation/idealization	Humor
Intellectualization	Self-discipline
Passive aggression	Sublimation
Projection	Suppression
Rationalization	
Repression	
Splitting self and others	

The outcome of the situation: *Michael and I didn't fight and I felt even closer to him. I was able to see his point of view and control my thoughts, feelings, and tendency to react negatively. I controlled the situation and myself.*

Identifying the connection between core content, activating event, defense mechanisms used, and outcome really helped Betty see the benefit of using healthy defense mechanisms. I encourage you to use the log for past, present, and possible future situations. You can download a copy of this log in

the summary for part 4 at http://www
.newharbinger.com/42730.

Defense Mechanisms Outcome Log

My core content of _____
was activated when _____

_____

I used the following defense
mechanisms (circle all the ones you
used).

Unhealthy Defense Mechanisms	Healthy Defense Mechanisms
Acting out	Altruism
Denial	Anticipation
Devaluation/idealization	Humor
Intellectualization	Self-discipline
Passive aggression	Sublimation
Projection	Suppression
Rationalization	
Repression	
Splitting self and others	

The outcome of the situation: _____

_____
_____
_____

As you move forward and pinpoint the events that activate your core content and the positive outcomes from using healthy defense mechanisms instead of unhealthy ones, you'll loosen the grip of your BPD. The exercises in this chapter are to be done many times; the process of doing them again and again will build your skill of choosing heathy defense mechanisms over unhealthy ones. As with all the others in this workbook, this skill is like roller skating: the more you do it, the better you'll get at it, until choosing healthy defense mechanisms becomes an automatic adaptive and healthy response pattern.

Building Blocks for the New You

Using the spaces below, pull together what you learned from this chapter so you can take this information with you.

The most helpful information I learned from this chapter:

1. _____
2. _____
3. _____

The skills that I want to practice:

1. _____
2. _____
3. _____

While going through this chapter, I was thinking _____, and it helped me to see that _____
_____

In the next chapter we're going to examine your internal love/hate conflict, so you can reduce the conflict and confusion you experience related to how you see yourself, feel about yourself, and think about yourself.

CHAPTER 19

Conquering the Internal Love/Hate Conflict

Your internal love/hate conflict is an inner battle between kindness and hatred, compassion and loathing, and the care and contempt you feel for yourself, the world, and those around you, including people who've hurt you and those who love you. The internal love/hate conflict creates confusion that breeds uncertainty and self-hatred and encourages negative beliefs, behaviors, and patterns. This confusion encompasses thoughts and images; things you say to yourself; how you see yourself; and how you see your past, present, and future. How you respond to this confusion can have a tremendous impact on your life.

In this chapter we're going to explore your internal love/hate conflict. The knowledge and skills you'll gain will lessen your confusion and conflict and strengthen your self-love, so that you can continue on this journey of growing beyond your BPD. The content in this chapter may bring up many issues about your past and feelings that you've not yet explored or haven't explored in a while. Don't forget to use the HELP steps, if you need them.

Defining Your Internal Love/Hate Conflict

Many individuals along the BPD spectrum are in a state of confusion related to self-hate and self-love, the elements that make up your internal love/hate conflict. Before you can conquer it, you have to know what it is. Tony explored the things he loved and hated about himself in order to get a handle on his own love/hate conflict.

What I Love About Myself	What I Hate About Myself
I'm kind and caring.	I'm not worth her time.
I'm smart and able.	I don't feel important.
I'm determined to succeed.	I give up.
I'm seeing myself differently.	I just keep hurting myself and others.

Tony's confusion fed his internal love/hate conflict, making it harder for him to engage in adaptive and healthy beliefs, behaviors, and patterns. Having awareness of this helped him reduce the confusion and conflict he'd been struggling with for so many years.

Let's start you on the path to reducing your struggle with your love/hate conflict. Be as honest as you can and make sure you're accessing your authentic view (chapter 16) and your adaptive and healthy hopes, beliefs, and wishes (chapter 17).

What I Love About Myself	What I Hate About Myself

Now that you've defined what makes up your internal love/hate conflict, the next step is to replace the confusion with strategies that build self-love and weaken self-hate.

Strategies of Self-Hate and Self-Love

Below are strategies that people use that contribute to the internal love/hate conflict. These are plans of action that influence how you see yourself, others, and situations. Place a checkmark next to the strategies you engage in. You may mark both the self-hate and self-love strategies in the same category. This is common; the strategies you use can be based on the many different thoughts, feelings, and memories that influence how you see yourself and the world, and how you act and react in various situations.

Self-Hate	Self-Love
☐ <u>Preventing patience</u> Demanding an immediate response to the emotions you feel, which gives you a false belief that if you've expressed them, you've controlled them.	☐ <u>Practicing patience</u> Recognizing your drive to respond. Reminding yourself that you don't have to respond immediately. Allowing yourself to slow down, explore (What emotions, thoughts, and images are coming to my mind?), reason (What are my expectations?), and respond using a clear head uncluttered by confusion.
☐ <u>Allowing hateful thoughts</u> Unquestioningly accepting thoughts as truth, especially the negative ones. Allowing hateful thoughts about yourself, others, and the world to come at you quickly and sharply, without defense.	☐ <u>Challenging hateful thoughts</u> Questioning how accurate your hateful thoughts are. Asking what their basis in reality is. What proves them wrong? Using the "three Cs" (Creed, Reisweber, and Beck 2011): catch your thoughts that came before your emotions, check how accurate and useful they are, and change them to be more accurate and helpful ones.
☐ <u>Empowering demons</u> Accepting your demons without question and giving in to them without confronting them. Demons are those things you tell yourself that are related to your core content; they degrade you, judge you harshly, and encourage a negative view of yourself, others, and the world around you.	☐ <u>Deconstructing demons</u> Reminding yourself that your demons are a negative part of your core content that's talking to you, encouraging your BPD and negative beliefs, behaviors, and patterns. Facing your demons is to confront them; to explore their reality while being kind, curious, and respectful of yourself; and to take them apart and to see how inaccurate they really are.

☐ Holding on to self-hatred	☐ Holding on to self-love
Allowing self-hatred to control you when you feel you've done something bad or wrong, which encourages a cycle of self-abuse, confusion, and conflict, causing feelings of abuse and shame.	Recognizing what is good, kind, caring, and compassionate about yourself; examining what you did that was bad or wrong; and giving yourself permission to make mistakes and errors, because everyone does; and making amends in order to forgive yourself.
☐ Self-blaming	☐ Forgiving myself
Focusing on mistakes you've made in your life, the evidence you use when you put yourself on trial to prove that your negative core content and BPD are correct. Beating yourself up to feel bad enough and motivated enough to do good things, even though in reality this strategy doesn't work.	Taking a step back and looking at the big picture of your mistake. Asking yourself, "Would I condemn someone as much as I'm condemning myself for the same mistake?" Recognizing that everyone is allowed to make mistakes, even you, and making amends for it. Doing good for others, if you can't do so for the person related to the mistake you made. Once you engage in reparation, letting go of your mistake without expectation of recognition or return for the good deed.
☐ Dismissing compassion	☐ Cradling compassion
Showing compassion to others before you show it yourself, which encourages you to see yourself as unworthy of compassion, understanding, and acceptance. Holding yourself to unrealistic expectations that your negative core content and early experiences have perpetuated, which breeds intolerance and self-hatred.	Fostering and demonstrating compassion and empathy for yourself, when you need it, as you would treat a child you love and care for.
☐ Disregarding the now	☐ Being here and now
Remaining focused on the rearview mirror, not the direction you're headed—that is, what's going on right here, right now.	Bringing awareness to the here and now, to the present moment, by digging up the roots that have kept you locked in place for too long. Recognizing that you can't impact your past, but you can impact the present, the here and now that's filled with options and choices, with adaptive and healthy strategies.
☐ Expectations of perfection	☐ Embracing good enough
Feeling the need to be perfect, perfectly stable or perfectly broken, and so on, and seeing yourself, others, and situations only one way—your way without error or deviation.	Holding on to the idea that you, others, and the situations you're in are good enough to give you what you need and want, even if they're not exactly how you imagined them to be. Remembering that the people and situations you compare yourself to are also flawed and imperfect.

Self-Hate	Self-Love
☐ <u>Dismissing support</u> Isolating and pushing away people who want to help you grow and develop. Building a system around yourself that undermines your belief in yourself, makes you question the sincerity of those who want to lift you up, and reinforces your confusion and conflict, leaving you off-balance. When you dismiss support, there's no one around to challenge your self-hatred, so it's all you see.	☐ <u>Embracing support</u> Recognizing your worth and creating a support system that does the same. Embracing the people in this system, who should be kind, caring, compassionate, tolerant, dependable, and consistent, and accepting their kindness, not challenging it. Letting go of unhealthy people who encourage your negative core content and don't provide you the support you deserve.
☐ <u>Encouraging self-hate</u> Automatically seeing only one side of yourself, the one that's dark, chaotic, destructive, and hurtful. Dismissing positive statements from yourself and others, seeing success as luck, and resisting others who try to help you grow and develop. This strategy can seem like a familiar friend who you've been journeying with for a long time, but the road trip you've been on has been filled with only bad experiences of blame and self-loathing that have kept you in a cycle of self-hate.	☐ <u>Encouraging self-love</u> Acknowledging and embracing what's good about you, such as your caring, compassionate, creative, and powerful nature. Recognizing what makes you unique and special, including that you're a survivor of your experiences. Accepting when someone acknowledges these aspects of you, and using that information to lift yourself up—these acknowledgments are like souvenirs from a wonderful trip.

Examining self-hate and self-love strategies can bring up a lot of thoughts, feelings, and memories. Don't be hard on yourself if you tend to use more self-hate strategies. You learned these while growing up, as your core content and BPD were developing. Take a moment to explore the thoughts, feelings, and memories that are linked to your internal love/hate conflict using the space below. This exercise can help you see the impact this conflict has on you and your world, giving you the understanding to help you overcome self-hate and build self-love.

When I look at the self-hate strategies I marked, I feel _____

When I look at the self-hate strategies I marked, I think and remember _____

When I look at the self-love strategies I marked, I feel _____

When I look at the self-love strategies I marked, I think and remember _____

Conquering Self-Hate and Encouraging Self-Love

Before you conquer self-hate, it's important to link your self-hate and self-love strategies with your core content. This insight will help you see the driving force behind the confusion that comes from your internal love/hate conflict. Your negative core content areas tend to be linked to self-hate strategies, whereas your positive core content areas are more likely to be associated with self-love strategies. These core content areas are in constant conflict to gain control over how you see yourself, others, and the world.

The following worksheet is going to help you make these connections, which will reduce the conflict you feel going forward. Place a checkmark next to the self-hate or self-love strategy you use. If you use both, then mark both. Then write the associated core content areas in the box you think they're related to. If you don't feel that either strategy relates to a core content area, then leave the space blank and move on to the next strategy. You might find it useful to revisit the roots of your core content that you uncovered in chapter 15.

Core Content and Self-Hate/Self-Love Worksheet

Self-Hate and Self-Love Strategies	
☐ Preventing patience ☐ Practicing patience Core content: _____	☐ Dismissing compassion ☐ Cradling compassion Core content: _____
☐ Allowing hateful thoughts ☐ Challenging hateful thoughts Core content: _____	☐ Disregarding the now ☐ Being here and now Core content: _____
☐ Empowering demons ☐ Deconstructing demons Core content: _____	☐ Expectations of perfection ☐ Embracing good enough Core content: _____
☐ Holding on to self-hatred ☐ Holding on to self-love Core content: _____	☐ Dismissing support ☐ Embracing support Core content: _____
☐ Self-blaming ☐ Forgiving myself Core content: _____	☐ Encouraging Self-Hate ☐ Encouraging Self-Love Core content: _____

Making the connection between your core content and your self-hate and self-love strategies is a big step, but there's one more step to take: pulling it all together. Before you do this, let's look at an example of Tony's.

Self-Hate and Self-Love Strategies
☑ Preventing patience
☐ Practicing patience
Core content: Worthlessness, feeling invisible

Tony determined that his core content of "worthlessness" and "feeling invisible" was linked to the strategy of "preventing patience." The intense emotions he had related to this content, such as believing he'd never be valued, caused him to react immediately in situations. He engaged in default negative beliefs, behaviors, and patterns, such as calling his girlfriends over and over again until they answered (a form of the "preventing patience" strategy), which pushed them away. He'd then use this as evidence of his worthlessness, leading to feelings of self-hate. Once Tony had explored how his core content influenced the self-hate strategy he often used, he identified ways he could respond differently.

My core content of *worthlessness and feeling invisible* is linked to the self-hate strategy of *preventing patience.*

How my core content influences my use of this strategy: *I become impatient when I feel forced to respond right away, like I can't wait. When Pam doesn't answer my call, I feel invisible and worthless. I feel like I'm going to lose control of the situation and myself, and other people will control me.*

I will do it differently by using the strategy of *practicing patience:When I feel the urge to respond immediately, that is my core content of worthlessness and feeling invisible talking. I hear my mom in my head telling me negative things, but I control who I listen to and what I do. I will take deep breaths, reexamine the situation, weigh the pros and cons, and think about what it is I want in the end. I'll determine what will help me and what won't hurt me.*

Tony was able to see what drove him to use self-hate strategies. Once he had this awareness, he was able to clearly identify techniques that promoted self-love. You can as well. Using the following worksheet, identify the core content areas that are associated with the self-hate strategies you use, describe how your core content influences the strategies you use, and then describe how you'll do it differently using a self-love strategy instead. You'll see that I've included a prompt for *every* self-love and self-hate strategy. This is purposeful. Even if you're not using a particular self-hate strategy, I'd like you to try to imagine yourself using the counter self-love strategy in some situation in life. So please try not to leave any of the self-love strategies blank. You can download a copy of this worksheet in the summary for part 4 at http://www.newharbinger.com/42730.

Conquering Self-Hate and Encouraging Self-Love

My core content of _____ is linked to the self-hate strategy of *preventing patience.*

How my core content influences my use of this strategy: _____

I will do it differently by using the strategy of *practicing patience:* _____

_____

My core content of _____ is linked to the self-hate strategy of *allowing hateful thoughts.*

How my core content influences my use of this strategy: _____

_____

I will do it differently by using the strategy of *challenging hateful thoughts:* _____

_____

My core content of _____ is linked to the self-hate strategy of *empowering demons.*

How my core content influences my use of this strategy: _____

I will do it differently by using the strategy of *deconstructing demons:* _____

_____

My core content of _____ is linked to the self-hate strategy of *holding on to self-hatred.*

How my core content influences my use of this strategy: _____

I will do it differently by using the strategy of *holding on to self-love:* _____

My core content of _____ is linked to the self-hate strategy of *self-blaming.*

How my core content influences my use of this strategy: _____

I will do it differently by using the strategy of *forgiving myself:* _____

My core content of _____ is linked to the self-hate strategy of *dismissing compassion.*

How my core content influences my use of this strategy:

_____

I will do it differently by using the strategy of *cradling compassion:*

_____

My core content of _____ is linked to the self-hate strategy of *disregarding the now.*

How my core content influences my use of this strategy: _____

_____

I will do it differently by using the strategy of *being here and now:* _____

_____

My core content of _____ is linked to the self-hate strategy of *expectations of perfection.*

How my core content influences my use of this strategy: _____

_____

I will do it differently by using the strategy of *embracing good enough:* _____

My core content of _____ is linked to the self-hate strategy of *dismissing support.*

How my core content influences my use of this strategy: _____

I will do it differently by using the strategy of *embracing support:* _____

My core content of _____ is linked to the self-hate strategy of *encouraging self-hate.*

How my core content influences my use of this strategy: _____

I will do it differently by using the strategy of *encouraging self-love:* _____

This exercise has hopefully helped you to see ways to add self-love strategies to your life. Doing so will lessen the conflict you feel and reduce the confusion that is inherent to BPD, which has had you in its grip for too long. The more you practice self-love strategies, the more powerful and helpful they'll become.

Building Blocks for the New You

Using the spaces below, pull together what you learned from this chapter so you can take this information with you.

The most helpful information I learned from this chapter:

1. _____

2. _____

3. _____

The skills that I want to practice:

1. _____

2. _____

3. _____

While going through this chapter, I was thinking _____, and it helped me to see that _____

Having an awareness of your internal love/hate conflict will empower you to better control its content and how you see yourself, others, and situations in life. All of the skills you've learned in this book have prepared you to give up your old ways and embrace the new ones—the subject of the next chapter.

CHAPTER 20

Letting Go and Moving On with the New You

In this workbook so far, you've examined and learned strategies for controlling how your core content affects your life and how you see yourself, others, and situations. This process has helped you develop and strengthen methods for moving beyond your BPD. This chapter is going to continue that trend. You're going to learn more strategies for letting go of the old ways while embracing the adaptive and healthy patterns that encourage growth, build empowerment, and strengthen the control you have over your life, especially when your core content is activated.

Growing from Then to Now

Think back to what prompted you to pick up this workbook. What was going on in your life at that time? Defining a clear distinction between then and now is very important. It will help you see the gains you've made, as well as strengthen the perspective that you can overcome BPD. Let's take a look at the distinction Betty made between her old ways and her new ways.

My old ways *led me to be suspicious, upset, and angry when things did not go as I expected them to or felt they should. This caused my core content to explode. I would feel a sense of abandonment and emptiness, like I had lost my integrity and resolve and that there was nothing I could do about it, except to respond in a desperate way before I drowned in my emotions. My old ways destroyed my relationships, while clouding how I saw myself and the people in my life. I cut myself and slept with different people, trying to make myself feel better, but none of it worked. This cycle wouldn't* stop, and I was in an emotional tornado that was ripping through my life.

My new ways allow me to breathe. I now know what my buttons, triggers, and beliefs, behaviors, and patterns are. When I feel abandoned and empty, I can explore these feelings, control them, and change them—clearly seeing how my life really is and that my wishes and fears don't have to control me and confuse me. I can use healthy defenses and build healthy relationships with myself and other people. These are filled with love and connection that allow me to grow. From this growth I've been able to paint a picture of a future that I never thought was possible, but it is, and I own it. And I feel wrapped in integrity and resolve to achieve good things in my life.

Betty was able to see where she was "then" without attacking herself, and she was able to use it to see where she is now. She sees her life filled with potential and hope, and she recognizes that by using adaptive and healthy beliefs, behaviors, and patterns she has more control over herself and the way she sees others and life's situations.

Now it's your turn to explore your old and new ways. In the spaces below, describe your old and new ways as you see them today and how they impact how you view yourself, others, and situations. Be as detailed as you can, and try not to hold back. Don't judge yourself for where you were. Use where you are to encourage and empower yourself for the future.

My old ways _____

_____

_____

_____

My new ways _____

_____

_____

_____

Writing out your old and new ways helps reinforce and clarify your resolve to grow beyond your BPD using adaptive and healthy beliefs, behaviors, and patterns. It can also help you to reinterpret your core content and what it means when it shows up in your life.

Core Content Signals

As you've gone through this workbook, you've explored and challenged your core content, and you're likely seeing it differently now. Whereas in the past your core content dictated your behavior and how you responded to people and situations that triggered you, now it signals you—with feelings and thoughts—when it's triggered, so you can evaluate and determine the best course of action for yourself.

Betty used to respond immediately when people or situations triggered her core content. But, as she went through treatment, she began to recognize that her core content was sending her signals—feelings and thoughts—that she could use to make a choice about which beliefs, behaviors, and patterns she wanted to engage in. Betty used to get very angry, isolate herself, look for romantic partners, and cut herself when her core content was triggered. Now when she's triggered, she has several helpful skills to choose from, such as mindfulness to slow her mind down and explore her beliefs, thoughts, and feelings. As a result, she can approach the triggering person or event with a calm, collected, and clear mind that's not distorted by BPD and unhealthy patterns. She's empowered and more in control of herself, which give her flexibility in the situations she finds herself in. Making sense of her core content and her behavior has allowed her to get what she needs and wants out of her life.

Use the spaces below to describe how your view of your core content, and your relationship with it, has changed. Be as descriptive as you can, and use this opportunity to reinforce the foundation of understanding you've developed regarding your core content. Please use blank sheets of paper if you run out of space, or you can download a copy of this exercise at http://www.n ewharbinger.com/42730. Write as much as you need to. This is an exercise you should do on a regular basis.

My core content used to make me

My core content signals are _____

_____

_____

When I receive signals from my core content, I use these adaptive and healthy beliefs, behaviors, and patterns:

_____

_____

_____

Hopefully answering these questions has offered you greater clarity about your core content, allowing you to embrace it and use it to your advantage. That is personal power and control. As you go forward and grow, it's important to be aware of the tendency to *regress,* to go back to those old ways. To resist this temptation, it's helpful to identify what might cause you to revert back to negative and unhealthy beliefs, behaviors, and patterns.

Moves Me Forward or Holds Me Back

In this exercise you'll examine what moves you forward and what holds you back. Having an awareness of these influences can help you make clear choices that will maintain your personal growth and increase your sense of control and empowerment, increasing the likelihood that you'll get your wants and needs met. This exercise certainly had that effect on Betty. Here's how she filled out the exercise.

Who discourages my adaptive and healthy beliefs, behaviors, and patterns?

Robert, my mother, and some of my friends

What do they do that holds me back?

They trigger my core content and seem to be empowered by my struggles and pain. My ex used to call me names, and my mother still doesn't seem to want to be a part of my life. She wasn't very nice to me the few times we spoke recently.

How can I reduce their impact?

I can distance myself from them. I can spend less time with them, or no time. If I'm around them and my core content is sending signals to me, I can use adaptive and healthy response patterns to control or leave the situation.

Who supports me in my efforts to change my beliefs, behaviors, and patterns?

Michael is a strong supporter of my growth. Many of my coworkers now spend more time with me and ask for advice regarding patients. My therapy group encourages me, empowering me to continue to work on personal control.

What can I do to encourage those who support me?

I can be honest and open with them about my feelings and struggles. I can continue to use healthy and adaptive response patterns to strengthen our relationships.

How can I strengthen their positive influence?

I'll continue to use my venting journal to self-soothe, and I'll use adaptive and healthy beliefs, behaviors, and patterns when I'm triggered and my emotional buttons are pushed. I'm dedicated to practicing my skills, building my empowerment, and encouraging and allowing these positive people to be in my life and close to me.

You've made many of the same gains that Betty has. Using the spaces below, explore who and what move you forward or might hold you back. Be as descriptive as you can, and take your time as you examine these different areas of yourself and your world. This is a great activity to do many times throughout the year, as your world will change, and the people in it may change as well. You can download a copy of this worksheet at http://www.newharbinger.com/42730.

Who discourages my adaptive and healthy beliefs, behaviors, and patterns?

_____

_____

What do they do that holds me back?

_____

_____

How can I reduce their impact?

Who supports me in my efforts to change my beliefs, behaviors, and patterns?

What can I do to encourage those who support me?

How can I strengthen their positive influence?

Empowering Yourself

Empowerment is a very big part of continuing to grow beyond your BPD and resisting regression. In this exercise you're going to identify words of empowerment and then use them to develop empowerment statements, which can help you maintain your successes and build upon them.

Go through the list of words of empowerment below and circle the ones that describe you now that you're growing beyond your BPD and have greater personal control thanks to your adaptive and healthy beliefs, behaviors, and patterns. They should make you feel stronger, confident, and more in control of your life. If there are words you're not familiar with, don't worry about it. Take a few moments to look them up. This will build your empowerment vocabulary, helping you to refine and expand your sense of how accomplished, captivating, generous, soothing, resolute, and pleasant you are. If you feel the list is missing some empowerment words, write them in.

After you've circled the words that describe you, complete the empowerment statements that follow. Do your best to make them as specific to you and your world as you can, and try to use more than one word of empowerment to complete each statement. Have fun with this exercise! Allow yourself to get absorbed by your amazing growth, determination, and psychological health. You can download a blank copy of this worksheet in the summary for part 4 at http://www.new harbinger.com/42730, so you can review and revise your statements again and again as you grow beyond your BPD.

Able

Accomplished

Achieved

Alive

Ambitious

Awesome

Beautiful

Brilliant

Captivating

Clearly

Compelling

Conqueror

Controller

Courageous

Creative

Daring

Determined

Discovered

Driven

Dutiful

Eager

Energetic

Energized

Enjoyment

Excited

Exciting

Exuberant

Fabulous

Faith

Fearless

Focused

Fun

Generous

Goodwill

Grace

Growth

Happiness

Harmonious

Healthy

Honest

Hope

Illumination

Imaginative

Incredible

Insightful

Inspirational

Inspired

Intrepid

Joy

Jubilant

Kick-ass

Kind

Lively

Love

Lovely

Luminous

Magnificent

Mighty

Outrageous

Outstanding

Passionate

Patient

Peaceful

Persistent

Persuasive

Pleasant

Powerful

Purposeful

Quality

Radiance

Released

Renewed

Resilient

Resolute

Soothed

Strong

Thriving

Transforming

Unlimited

Vigorous

Visionary

Worthwhile

Worthy

Zealous

_____

_____

_____

_____

_____

_____

_____

Empowerment Statements

I am (add word or words of empowerment) _____ because I _____

_____

_____

I see myself as (add word or words of empowerment) _____ because I _____

_____

_____

I feel (add word or words of empowerment) _____ because I _____

_____

_____

I will be (add word or words of empowerment) _____ because I _____

_____

_____

You can use the results of this exercise to make an audio or video recording of yourself saying your empowerment statements, or you can include them in your venting journal. If one of your empowerment statements stands out, take a picture of it with your phone and save it, or maybe decorate it with an app to personalize it. Make this statement a part of who you are today, to take with you as you continue to grow. This is definitely not a "one and done" exercise, but something you can continue to use to build on your success and to encourage yourself to continue to achieve wonderful things.

You've grown beyond your old negative beliefs, behaviors, and patterns, and you've developed new ways of seeing yourself and the world. Your adaptive and healthy skills have opened up a world of new and exciting opportunities. You're in control, and you make the decisions that influence how you live life, not your BPD.

Building Blocks for the New You

Using the spaces below, pull together what you learned from this chapter so you can take this information with you.

The most helpful information I learned from this chapter:

1. _____

2. _____

3. _____

The skills that I want to practice:

1. _____

2. _____

3. _____

While going through this chapter, I was thinking _____, and it helped me to see that _____

_____

In the next, and last, part of the workbook, we'll explore strategies for maintaining your gains and continuing to move forward beyond your BPD. Before you move on to part 5, I recommend that you go through the summary for part 4 that's available for download at http://www.newharbinger.com/42730. This summary pulls together the concepts, activities, and exercises from part 4, and it will strengthen what you've learned in order to keep those old negative beliefs, behaviors, and patterns out of your life.

PART 5

Maintaining Your Success and Personal Power

CHAPTER 21

Maintaining Your Gains

You've made incredible gains with your BPD! You're now able to better control what once pulled you down and held you back. This last part of the workbook is going to help you maintain your gains and avoid falling back into those discarded BPD beliefs, behaviors, and patterns.

In the previous chapter I introduced the concept of regression, which happens when a person falls back into those old beliefs, behaviors, and patterns of BPD. Stress is one of the major causes for people to regress, and it can wear away at a person's *self-acceptance,* which is a recognition of personal strengths and weaknesses; an acknowledgement of skills, talents, and worth; and a love for yourself despite flaws and past behaviors and actions. There's no way to have a stress-free life, but you can control the impact stress has on you and your world—and on your self-acceptance—by understanding it and developing skills to cope with it. You've already learned many skills in this workbook that will help you combat and reduce the impact of stress, so in this chapter we're going to examine the different types of stress and focus on strengthening and maintaining your self-acceptance.

Types of Stress

We're going to review five types of stress, each of which has its own unique presence and impact on you and your self-acceptance. These types of stress can occur together, in various forms, and in varying amounts.

Type of Stress	Definition	Impact on Self-Acceptance and Ways to Deal with It
Time limited	This is the most common form of stress. It occurs for a limited time, but the stress can be intense. The stress only lasts as long as the stressor is present. Examples include being stuck in traffic or having a one-time argument with your significant other or child. Time-limited stress can be motivational; for example, you might experience stress about an upcoming job interview or date, so you prepare for it in order to give a good first impression.	This type of stress is the least likely to cause you to regress or to wear away your self-acceptance. You can use this stress to build your self-acceptance by acknowledging your strength and skills when you overcome and manage it.
Environmental	This type of stress occurs naturally in your environment. Examples include an annoying noise outside that you can't stop, a rainy day when you wanted to be outside, or a crowded movie theater on the opening day of a movie you want to see.	Environmental stress will most likely have little negative impact on your self-acceptance because you know you didn't create the stressor. However, you do determine how you handle the stress. Handling it with adaptive and healthy patterns reinforces self-acceptance.
Blended	These are stressful events that happen one after the other. For example, let's say you're in a car accident, then you're late to pick your child up from school, and then you miss a phone interview for an upcoming job.	As the pressure of blended stress increases, it can impact self-acceptance by causing you to regress to old BPD patterns. Using adaptive and healthy patterns and managing each stressor as it arises can help you avoid this.

Type of Stress	Definition	Impact on Self-Acceptance and Ways to Deal with It
Continuous	This is stress that continues for an extended period of time. Examples include living in poverty, living with untreated medical or psychological issues (such as BPD), or being in an unhappy marriage, job, or career.	This type of stress can have the greatest negative impact on psychological and physical health and self-acceptance. It feels like a wearing away of your adaptive and healthy patterns. When continuous stress occurs, it's time to review the skills you've learned, as well as the summaries of this book, to maintain and reinforce your gains and to make the changes you need to make. (The summaries are available for download at http://www.newharbinger.com/42730.)
Historical	This is stress that happened a long time ago but still causes you concern. Examples include child abuse, the death of a loved one, or being abandoned by parent.	This stress once haunted you and kept your self-acceptance at a distance. It may take random jabs at your self-acceptance, but you're probably too strong for it to impact you much, now that you've mastered your core content and response patterns. Keep using your adaptive and healthy patterns and you'll limit the destructive effects of this stress type.

Now that we've defined the five types of stress, how they can impact self-acceptance, and ways to combat them, you're ready to identify the types of stress you experience or you feel you're likely to experience. Let's take a look at Tony's types of stress first.

Stress Type: Time Limited

1. *At work my computer password expired and I had to wait for the IT person to give me another one.*

2.   *I dropped my cell phone and the screen cracked, so I had to go to the store and replace it.*
3.   *I had to pick up my girlfriend Julie from work, but I had to get gas, so I was late.*

Stress Type: Historical

1.   *My mom didn't give me the attention I wanted, and she neglected me.*
2.   *I didn't follow through with baseball, and I was really good at it.*

Once Tony received his new password, exchanged his cell phone, and picked up Julie, his time-limited stress was relieved. These experiences did not negatively impact his self-acceptance; in fact, they bolstered it because he handled them well, with confidence and self-control. His historical stress still causes him concern, but these individual stressors, which are also part of his core content, don't have the same impact they once did. The stress he feels from these is much lower than the time-limited stress he felt, because the historical stress is something that's been present for a long time, and he's dealt with it and adapted to it, limiting its impact.

Now it's your turn to identify and describe your stress. In the spaces below, describe the different types of stress you experience. As you're identifying them, consider where the stress is coming from, the impact it has on you, and who may be causing or contributing to it. Be as descriptive as you can, and if you don't have three examples for each type of stress, that's fine. If you have more than three, you can download a copy of this worksheet in the summary for part 5 at http://www.newharbinger.com/42730. The goal is to increase your awareness of which types of stress are present, or likely to be present, in your life.

Identifying Your Types of Stress

Stress Type: Time Limited

1. _____
   _____
2. _____
   _____
3. _____
   _____

Stress Type: Environmental

1. _____
   _____
2. _____
   _____
3. _____
   _____

Stress Type: Blended

1. _____
2. _____
   _____
3. _____
   _____

Stress Type: Continuous

1. _____
   _____
2. _____
   _____
3. _____
   _____

Stress Type: Historical

1. _____
   _____
2. _____
   _____
3. _____
   _____

Identifying your types of stress will help you pinpoint where it's coming from, its impact on you, and who may be causing or contributing to it. This important information can help you prepare for when it arises, reduce its impact before it can overwhelm you, and lessen the likelihood of you regressing back to old beliefs, behaviors, and patterns.

Maintaining Your Self-Acceptance

Just like your BPD used to do, stress feeds off your emotions, which intensifies its strength and makes it harder to control. Over time stress can wear away at your self-acceptance and put you at risk for regression. You can maintain your self-acceptance by using some of the skills you've learned in this workbook, such as managing emotional button responses (chapter 10), replacing behaviors in high-risk situations (chapter 11), using imagery for empowering relationship habits (chapter 14), using your authentic view cycle (chapter 16), using healthy defense mechanisms (chapter 18), and so on.

The following exercise will help you plan out your resistance to regression. First, you'll identify your types of stress and then determine what you can do to maintain your self-acceptance using the skills you've learned in this workbook. As you complete this exercise, keep your core content and response patterns in mind, the tools you use to master and control them, and how stress may influence them. You can download a copy of this worksheet in the summary for part 5 at http://www.newharbinger.com/4273 0.

When I experience (add type of stress) _____, I think about _____

_____

When I experience this stress, I feel _____

_____

When I experience this stress, I behave in these ways: _____

_____

I will maintain my self-acceptance by (add skills you can use) _____

_____

When I experience (add type of stress) _____, I think about _____

_____

When I experience this stress, I feel _____

_____

When I experience this stress, I behave in these ways: _____

_____

I will maintain my self-acceptance by (add skills you can use) _____

_____

_____

Sustaining Your Growth

Using the spaces below, pull together what you learned from this chapter so you can take this information with you.

The most helpful information I learned from this chapter:

1. _____

2. _____

3. _____

The skills that I want to practice:

1. _____

2. _____

3. _____

While going through this chapter, I was thinking _____, and it helped me to see that _____

_____

_____

Identifying the types of stress you experience and how they impact your thoughts, feelings, and behaviors empowers you to have greater control over how you experience and respond to them. Controlling how you handle stress will help you sustain your level of self-acceptance and clearly see your personal strengths and weaknesses; recognize your skills, talents, and worth; and accept yourself despite your flaws and past behaviors and actions. This *is* acceptance of who you are beyond the grip of your BPD.

CHAPTER 22

Life Beyond Your BPD

This may be the end of the workbook, but it's not the end of your journey growing beyond your BPD. You now have the knowledge to embrace your empowerment; the skills to go forward without being held back; and adaptive and healthy beliefs, behaviors, and patterns to maintain your gains.

Before I sign off, please take a moment and identify what you learned and what you'll be taking with you as you continue to grow beyond your BPD. It's a way of looking back before moving forward.

In part 1, I learned that BPD is:

_____

_____

_____

In part 2, I learned that my first steps toward growth are: _____

In part 3, I learned that to change my BPD patterns and behaviors I need to: _____

In part 4, I learned that the new me has the power to: _____

In part 5, I learned that to maintain my self-acceptance I will: _____

To resist regressing, managing stress and sustaining your gains and self-acceptance is going to be important as you move forward. To help strengthen what you've learned, there's a summary available for download at h ttp://www.newharbinger.com/42730. This summary pulls together the concepts, activities, and exercises from part 5 of the workbook, so I highly recommend that you take the time to go through it.

Congratulate the New You!

You have reached an incredible milestone in your life. Take a moment and write yourself a congratulations letter saying how proud you are of what you've achieved and for the successes you've had. Write about the parts of yourself that you admire and love, and wish yourself well as you go forward into a world full of opportunities with strength, personal power, and control.

Dear (your name) _____, I want to say that _____

EPILOGUE

Letter from Dr. Fox

When I conclude treatment with one of my clients, I like to give them a transitional object, something that provides psychological comfort. For a child, it can be a security blanket, or for an adult it can be a family heirloom or object of great importance that makes them feel safe and secure.

As I finished writing this workbook, I was thinking about what I could give you. What's your transitional object? Then it hit me! This workbook, with all your writings and truths, is your transitional object. It's as much a part of you as the knowledge, perceptions, and skills you're taking with you. Take this workbook and put it somewhere you can see it. Going forward, let it remind you of where you are and what you've accomplished. Remember, if you find yourself challenged down the road, open it up and use it to get back on track.

You have my fullest respect and admiration for all you've accomplished. Respectfully,

Daniel J. Fox

References

Agrawal, H.R., J. Gunderson, B.M. Holmes, and K. Lyons-Ruth. 2004. "Attachment Studies with Borderline Patients: A Review." *Harvard Review of Psychiatry* 12 (2): 94–104.

Ahmad A., N. Ramoz, P. Thomas, R. Jardri, and P. Gorwood. 2014. "Genetics of Borderline Personality Disorder: Systematic Review and Proposal of an Integrative Model." *Neuroscience and Biobehavioral Reviews* 40: 6–19.

APA (American Psychiatric Association). 2013. *Diagnostic and Statistical Manual of Mental Disorders.* 5th ed. Washington, DC: APA.

Ball, J.S., and P.S. Links. 2009. "Borderline Personality Disorder and Childhood Trauma: Evidence for a Causal Relationship." *Current Psychiatry Report* 11 (1): 63–68.

Bartholomew, K., and L.M. Horowitz. 1991. "Attachment Styles Among Young

Adults: A Test of a Four-Category Model." *Journal of Personality and Social Psychology* 61 (2): 226–244.

Battle C.L., M.T. Shea, D.M. Johnson, S. Yen, C. Zlotnick, M.C. Zanarini, C.A. Sanislow, A.E. Skodol, J.G. Gunderson, C.M. Grilo, T.H. McGlashan, and L.C. Morey. 2004. "Childhood Maltreatment Associated with Adult Personality Disorders: Findings from the Collaborative Longitudinal Personality Disorders Study." *Journal of Personality Disorders* 18 (2): 193–211.

Benjamin, L.S. 1996. *Interpersonal Diagnosis and Treatment of Personality Disorders.* New York: Guilford Press.

Boily, M.C., R.F. Baggaley, L. Wang, B. Masse, R.G. White, R. Hayes, and M. Alary. 2009. "Heterosexual Risk of HIV-1 Infection Per Sexual Act: Systematic Review and Meta-Analysis of Observational Studies." *Lancet: Infectious Diseases* 9 (2): 118–129.

Bowlby, J. 1971. *Attachment and Loss.* Vol.1, Attachment. London: Penguin Books.

Bowlby, J. 1977. "The Making and Breaking of Affectional Bonds: I. Aetiology and Psychopathology in the Light of Attachment Theory." *British Journal of Psychiatry* 130: 201–210.

Chanen, A.M., and M. Kaess. 2012. "Developmental Pathways to Borderline Personality Disorder." *Current Psychiatry Report* 14 (1): 45–53.

Ciarrochi, J. 2004. "Relationships Between Dysfunctional Beliefs and Positive and Negative Indices of Well-Being: A Critical Evaluation of the Common Beliefs Survey-III." *Journal of Rational-Emotive and Cognitive-Behavior Therapy* 22 (3): 171–188.

Clark, D.A. 2014. "Cognitive Restructuring." In *The Wiley Handbook of Cognitive Behavioral Therapy,* edited by S.G. Hofmann. Chichester, UK: Wiley-Blackewll.

Coid, J., M. Yang, P. Tyrer, A. Roberts, and S. Ullrich. 2006 "Prevalence and Correlates of Personality Disorder in Great Britain." *British Journal of Psychiatry* 188: 423–431.

Creed, T.A., J. Reisweber, and A.T. Beck. 2011. *Cognitive Therapy for Adolescents in School Settings.* New York: Guilford Press.

Dahl, A.A. 1985. "Borderline Disorders—The Validity of the Diagnostic Concept." *Psychiatry Developments* 3 (2): 109–152.

Delavechia, T.R., M.L. Velasquez, E.P. Duran, L.S. Matsumoto, and I. Reis de Oliveira. 2016. "Changing Negative Core Beliefs with Trial-Based Thought Record." *Archives of Clinical Psychiatry* 43 (2): 31–33.

Dingfelder, S.F. 2004. "Treatment for the 'Untreatable': Despite the Difficult-to-Treat Reputation of Personality Disorders, Clinical Trials of Treatments Show Promise." *Monitor on Psychology* 35 (3): 46.

Distel, M.A., T.J. Trull, C.A. Derom, E.W. Thiery, M.A. Grimmer, N.G. Martin, G. Willemsen, and D.I. Boomsma. 2008. "Heritability of Borderline Personality Disorder Features Is Similar Across Three Countries." *Psychological Medicine* 38 (9): 1219–1229.

Elzy, M.B. 2011. "Examining the Relationship Between Childhood Sexual Abuse and Borderline Personality Disorder: Does Social Support Matter?" *Journal of Childhood Sexual Abuse* 20 (3): 284–304.

Fonagy, P., M. Target, and G. Gergely. 2000. "Attachment and Borderline Personality Disorder: A Theory and Some Evidence." *Psychiatric Clinics of North America* 23 (1): 103–122.

Goodman, M., D. Carpenter, C.Y. Tang, K.E. Goldstein, J. Avedon, N. Fernandez, K.A. Mascitelli, N.J. Blair, A.S. New, J. Triebwasser, L.J. Siever, and E.A. Hazlett. 2014. "Dialectical Behavior Therapy Alters Emotion Regulation and Amygdala Activity in Patients with Borderline Personality

Disorder." *Journal of Psychiatric Research* 57: 108–116.

Grant, B.F., S.P. Chou, R.B. Goldstein, B. Huang, F.S. Stinson, T.D. Saha, S.M. Smith, D.A. Dawson, A.J. Pulay, R.P. Pickering, and W.J. Ruan. 2008. "Prevalence, Correlates, Disability, and Comorbidity of DSM-IV Borderline Personality Disorder: Results from the Wave 2 National Epidemiologic Survey on Alcohol and Related Conditions." *Journal of Clinical Psychiatry* 69 (4): 533–545.

Gunderson, J.G. 1994. "Building Structure for the Borderline Construct." *Acta Psychiatrica Scandinavica* 89 (s379): 12–18.

Gunderson J.G., M.C. Zanarini, L.W. Choi-Kain, K.S. Mitchell, K.L. Jang, and J.I. Hudson. 2011. "Family Study of Borderline Personality Disorder and Its Sectors of Psychopathology." *Archives of General Psychiatry* 68 (7): 753–762.

Judd, P.H., and T.H. McGlashan. 2003. *A Developmental Model of Borderline*

Personality Disorder: Understanding Variations in Course and Outcome. Washington, DC: American Psychiatric Publishing.

Kraft, T.L., and S.D. Pressman. 2012. "Grin and Bear It: The Influence of Manipulated Facial Expression on the Stress Response." *Psychological Science* 23 (11): 1372–1378.

Lenzenweger, M.F., M.C. Lane, A.W. Loranger, and R.C. Kessler. 2007. "DSM-IV Personality Disorders in the National Comorbidity Survey Replication." *Biological Psychiatry* 62 (6): 553–564.

Levy, K.N., K.B. Meehan, K.M. Kelly, J.S. Reynoso, M. Weber, and O.F. Kernberg. 2006. "Change in Attachment Patterns and Reflective Function in a Randomized Control Trial of Transference-Focused Psychotherapy for Borderline Personality Disorder." *Journal of Consulting and Clinical Psychology* 74 (6): 1027–1040.

Linehan, M. 1993. *Cognitive-Behavioral Treatment of Borderline Personality Disorder.* New York: Guilford Press.

MacIntosh, H.B., N. Godbout, and N. Dubash. 2015. "Borderline Personality Disorder: Disorder of Trauma or Personality, a Review of the Empirical Literature." *Canadian Psychology* 56 (2): 227–241.

McGowan, A., H. King, F.F. Frankenburg, G. Fitzmaurice, and M.C. Zanarini. 2012. "The Course of Adult Experiences of Abuse in Patients with Borderline Personality Disorder and Axis II Comparison Subjects: A 10-Year Follow-Up Study." *Journal of Personality Disorders* 26 (2): 192–202.

Millon, T. 1996. *Disorders of Personality: DSM-IV and Beyond.* 2nd ed. New York: John Wiley and Sons.

Perry, J.C., M.D. Presniak, and T.R. Olson. 2013. "Defense Mechanisms in Schizotypal, Borderline, Antisocial, and Narcissistic Personality Disorders." *Psychiatry* 76 (1): 32–52.

Prochaska, J.O., C.C. DiClemente, and J.C. Norcross. 1992. "In Search of How People Change: Applications to Addictive Behaviors." *American Psychologist* 47 (9): 1102–1114.

Prochaska, J.O., J.C. Norcross, and C.C. DiClemente. 2013. "Applying the Stages of Change." *Psychotherapy in Australia* 19 (2): 10–15.

Reichborn-Kjennerud, T., E. Ystrom, M.C. Neale, S.H. Aggen, S.E. Mazzeo, G.P. Knudsen, K. Tambs, N.O. Czajkowski, and K.S. Kendler. 2013. "Structure of Genetic and Environmental Risk Factors for Symptoms of DSM-IV Borderline Personality Disorder." *Journal of the American Medical Association Psychiatry* 70 (11): 1206–1214.

Ryan, R.M., and E.L. Deci. 2002. "Overview of Self-Determination Theory: An Organismic-Dialectical Perspective." In *Handbook of Self-Determination Research,* edited by E.L. Deci and R.M. Ryan. Rochester, NY: University of Rochester Press.

Sala, M., E. Caverzasi, M. Lazzaretti, N. Morandotti, G. De Vidovich, E. Marraffini, F. Gambini, M. Isola, M. De Bona, G. Rambaldelli, G. d'Allio, F. Barale, F. Zappoli, and P. Brambilla. 2011. "Dorsolateral Prefrontal Cortex and Hippocampus Sustain Impulsivity and Aggressiveness in Borderline Personality Disorder." *Journal of Affective Disorders* 131 (1–3): 417–421.

Samuels, J., W.W. Eaton, O.J. Bienvenu III, C.H. Brown, P.T. Costa Jr., and G. Nestadt. 2002 "Prevalence and Correlates of Personality Disorders in a Community Sample." *British Journal of Psychiatry* 180: 536–542.

Soloff, P., J. Nutche, D. Goradia, and V. Diwadkar. 2008. "Structural Brain Abnormalities in Borderline Personality Disorder: A Voxel-Based Morphometry Study." *Psychiatry Research* 164 (3): 223–236.

Trull, T. J, S. Jahng, R.L. Tomko, P.K. Wood, and K.J. Sher. 2010. "Revised NESARC Personality Disorder Diagnoses: Gender, Prevalence, and Comorbidity

with Substance Dependence Disorders."
Journal of Personality Disorders 24 (4):
412–426.

Welch, S.S., and M.M. Linehan. 2002.
"High-Risk Situations Associated with
Parasuicide and Drug Use in Borderline
Personality Disorder." *Journal of
Personality Disorders* 16 (6): 561–569.

Yen, S., M.T. Shea, C.L. Battle, D.M.
Johnson, C. Zlotnick, R. Dolan-Sewell,
A.E. Skodol, C.M. Grilo, J.G. Gunderson,
C.A. Sanislow, M.C. Zanarini, D.S.
Bender, J.B. Rettew, and T.H.
McGlashan. 2002. "Traumatic Exposure
and Posttraumatic Stress Disorder in
Borderline, Schizotypal, Avoidant, and
Obsessive-Compulsive Personality
Disorders: Findings from the
Collaborative Longitudinal Personality
Disorders Study." *Journal of Nervous
and Mental Disease* 190 (8): 510–518.

Zanarini, M.C., F.R. Frankenburg, J.
Hennen, D.B. Reich, and K.R. Silk.
2005. "The McLean Study of Adult
Development (MSAD): Overview and
Implications of the First Six Years of

Prospective Follow-Up." *Journal of Personality Disorders* 19 (5): 505–523.

Zanarini, M.C., F.R. Frankenburg, D.B. Reich, and G.M. Fitzmaurice. 2010. "Time to Attainment of Recovery from Borderline Personality Disorder and Stability of Recovery: A 10-Year Prospective Follow-Up Study." *American Journal of Psychiatry* 167 (6): 663–667.

Zanarini, M.C., F.R. Frankenburg, D.B. Reich, and G.M. Fitzmaurice. 2016. "Fluidity of the Subsyndromal Phenomenology of Borderline Personality Disorder over 16 Years of Prospective Follow-Up." *American Journal of Psychiatry* 173 (7): 688–694.

Zanarini, M.C., F.R. Frankenburg, L. Yong, G. Raviola, D.B. Reich, J. Hennen, J.I. Hudson, and J.G. Gunderson. 2004. "Borderline Psychopathology in the First-Degree Relatives of Borderline and Axis II Comparison Probands." *Journal of Personality Disorders* 18 (5): 439–447.

Zanarini, M.C., L. Yong, F.R. Frankenburg, J. Hennen, D.B. Reich, M.F. Marino, and A.A. Vujanovic. 2002. "Severity or Reported Childhood Sexual Abuse and Its Relationship to Severity of Borderline Psychopathology and Psychosocial Impairment Among Borderline Inpatients." *Journal of Nervous and Mental Disease* 190 (6): 381–387.

Daniel J. Fox, PhD, is a licensed psychologist in Texas, an international speaker, and award-winning author. He has been specializing in the treatment and assessment of individuals with personality disorders for over fifteen years in the state and federal prison system, universities, and in private practice. His specialty areas include personality disorders, ethics, burnout prevention, and emotional intelligence. He has published several articles in these areas, and is author of *The Clinician's Guide to Diagnosis and Treatment of Personality Disorders, The Narcissistic Personality Disorder Toolbox,* and the award-winning *Antisocial, Borderline, Narcissistic and Histrionic Workbook.*

Fox has been teaching and supervising students for more than fifteen years at various universities across the United States, some of which include West Virginia University, Texas A&M University, University of Houston, Sam Houston State University, and Florida State University. He is currently an adjunct assistant professor at the University of Houston, and maintains a private practice that specializes in the assessment and treatment of individuals with complex psychopathology and personality disorders. Fox has given numerous workshops and seminars on ethics and personality disorders; personality disorders and crime; treatment solutions for treating clients along the antisocial, borderline, narcissistic, and histrionic personality spectrum; emotional intelligence; narcissistic personality disorder and its impact on children and partners; managing mental health within the prison system; and others. Fox maintains a website and is on social media to present various treatment interventions focused on working with and attenuating the symptomatology related to individuals along the antisocial, borderline, narcissistic, and histrionic personality spectrum. Learn more at www.drdfox.com.

FROM OUR PUBLISHER—

As the publisher at New Harbinger and a clinical psychologist since 1978, I know that emotional problems are best helped with evidence-based therapies. These are the treatments derived from scientific research (randomized controlled trials) that show what works. Whether these treatments are delivered by trained clinicians or found in a self-help book, they are designed to provide you with proven strategies to overcome your problem.

Therapies that aren't evidence-based—whether offered by clinicians or in books—are much less likely to help. In fact, therapies that aren't guided by science may not help you at all. That's why this New Harbinger book is based on scientific evidence that the treatment can relieve emotional pain.

This is important: if this book isn't enough, and you need the help of a skilled therapist, use the following resources to find a clinician trained in the evidence-based protocols appropriate for your problem. And if you need more support—a community that understands what you're going through and can show you ways to cope—resources for that are provided below, as well.

Real help is available for the problems you have been struggling with. The skills you can learn from evidence-based therapies will change your life.

Matthew McKay, PhD

Publisher, New Harbinger Publications

If you need a therapist, the following organization can help you find a therapist trained in dialectical behavior therapy (DBT).

Behavioral Tech, LLC
please visit www.behavioraltech.org **and click on** *Find a DBT Therapist.*

For additional support for patients, family, and friends, please contact the following:

BPD Central **Visit** www.bpdcentral.org

Treatment and Research Advancements
Association for Personality Disorder
(TARA)
Visit www.tara4bpd.org

For more new harbinger books,
visit www.newharbinger.com

MORE BOOKS *from*
NEW HARBINGER PUBLICATIONS

Back Cover Material

AN INDIVIDUALIZED APPROACH TO MANAGING YOUR BPD SYMPTOMS

If you've been diagnosed with borderline personality disorder (BPD), you may feel many emotions—including shock, shame, sadness, abandonment, emptiness, or even anger. You may also be tempted to research your diagnosis online, only to find doomsday scenarios and terrible prognoses everywhere you click. You should know that no person experiences BPD in the same way, and that you can manage this. This workbook will be your guide.

Rather than a one-size-fits-all treatment, this comprehensive workbook meets you where *you are* on your therapeutic journey. You'll find an integrated, evidence-based approach grounded in dialectical behavior therapy (DBT), acceptance and commitment therapy (ACT), cognitive behavioral therapy (CBT), and interpersonal therapy to help you manage your specific symptoms. You'll also gain a greater understanding of your BPD, uncover your emotional triggers, and discover your own personal motivators for positive change.

Your BPD doesn't have to define you. With this compassionate and practical guide, you'll be ready to face your BPD head-on, and take those important first steps toward lasting wellness.

"A must-have for those who want to understand, treat, and recover from borderline personality. Enthusiastically recommended!"
—LANE PEDERSON, PSYD, author of *The Expanded Dialectical Behavior Therapy Skills Training Manual*

DANIEL J. FOX, PhD, is a licensed psychologist in Texas, an international speaker, and award-winning author. He has been specializing in the treatment and assessment of individuals with personality disorders for over fifteen years.

Lightning Source UK Ltd.
Milton Keynes UK
UKHW042211081022
410031UK00006B/28